PINNACLE VIEW: TAKING YOUR BUSINESS ALL THE WAY TO THE TOP

PINNACLE VIEW: TAKING YOUR BUSINESS ALL THE WAY TO THE TOP

BY KIMBERLY HEATHCOTT

MANUSCRIPTS PRESS

COPYRIGHT © 2023 KIMBERLY HEATHCOTT
All rights reserved.

PINNACLE VIEW: TAKING YOUR BUSINESS ALL THE WAY TO THE TOP

ISBN
979-8-88926-756-0   *Paperback*
979-8-88926-757-7   *Ebook*

I dedicate this book to my mom.

You gave me a little blue suitcase when I was five to fill with books from the public library next door, sent me to a Montessori school so I could read them, and then took a job at my high school, which gave me access to an amazing library.

Delighting in all those words and stories filled my childhood and fueled my dreams. Thank you.

Contents

FOREWORD 11

INTRODUCTION 15

PART 1: STARTING THE CLIMB 23
   BARBIE DREAM HOUSE 25

   CLIENT PROBLEMS. 35

   PEOPLE MATTER. .47

   SERVANT LEADERSHIP. 57

   BLEEDING EDGE SYNDROME 67

PART 2: BRAVING THE ELEMENTS 79
   FINANCIAL CRISIS .81

   PROPERTY PERILS .91

   ICE WARS 101

   HOLIDAY MEALS 109

PART 3: FIGHTING THROUGH SETBACKS AND STRUGGLES 117
   PARKING LOT WARS 119

   UNHINGED 129

   UNDER PRESSURE. 137

   PERSONALITY, PRESSURE, AND PREDICAMENTS 147

   RANSOMED 159

PART 4: GAINING TRACTION ALL THE WAY TO THE TOP . . 169
    WINNING MEMPHIS STYLE 171
    SCALING THE HEIGHTS. 183
    THE PINNACLE. 193

PART 5: JOURNEYING DOWN 203
    THE DROP 205
    KUDZU 215
    DECISIONS 221

PART 6: SURVEYING THE VISTA 231
    REINVENTION 233
    REFRESHMENT. 239
    REFLECTIONS 245
    ACKNOWLEDGMENTS 253
    APPENDIX 255

"It's never too late to be what you might have been."

—ANONYMOUS

Foreword

I come from a long line of independent, resilient, and sincere women. These women have forged a path for me to look up to and follow.

It is important for daughters to have role models... I have many on both sides of my family.

I'll start with the one who imprinted her stamp on my life immeasurably: My mom, Kim Heathcott.

Sitting to one side of our family room, we had a chair and matching ottoman that were comfortable and not really aesthetically pleasing, but they still remained a constant piece of furniture in any house we occupied. The pattern and shape of the chair are a distant memory, yet the chair remained a visual anchor as I made the transition from childhood to adulthood. Because it was mom's chair, or as I perceived it, her throne.

When my brother and I came home from afternoon activities and sports, we always knew where to find my mom in the house. On the off chance she made it home before 06:00 p.m. on a weeknight—sometimes even weekends—we knew she would be in her chair working on something work-related on the laptop while we told her about our days or watched a movie as a family.

This scene was an example of what I came to understand to be a norm when my mom started her company. Mom worked harder than anyone I had ever or maybe will ever see. She barely slept, worked every weekend, and stayed up at night until she could finally convince herself to shut the laptop off. Someone who lacks context on who my mom is as a person and mother would assume this kind of behavior would make her hard or disengaged from her kids and family. Not my mom.

I grew up with my stay-at-home mom smocking my dresses and driving me to sleepovers and birthday parties. She devoted her time to her two kids, and we felt all of it. Not until later in life did we—as her kids—realize she had an entire business career before having kids. It makes sense... she is brilliant.

I was ten years old when my mom started her company. Family dinners and nights watching *American Idol* before bed slowly transitioned to later dinners after both of my parents came home from work.

From what I remember of my childhood, both of my parents have always bent over backward to ensure my brother and I felt as much love as possible. They raised us to be responsible and kind people.

No matter how crazy and chaotic work would get for her, my mom would always drive me to every out-of-town swim meet. She would emerge right on time to watch me race, screaming passionately and waiting after every swim to see me before returning to her folding chair that housed her laptop and hours of remaining work she had for the day.

That is what I admire most about her. She could be drowning in things to do or projects to finish, but nothing was too big to put aside to show up for her kids with a smile and her own words of encouragement when—no doubt—she was actually the one in need of a pep talk.

While my mom was not as present in things as she may have been if remaining a stay-at-home mom, I would not have gained as much from her as a role model as I have. I learned independence as a young child. Not because I was forced to but because she set an example to think and act for yourself but never strip empathy, intention, and time away from the relationships you value. Doing so chips away from your own character, and she never made anyone feel less loved and valued despite the stress she had placed on herself.

I look back on my childhood and my life now as a twenty-three-year-old woman and am thankful I have a mom I consider a best friend. She always has a listening ear for her kids. She has eagerness and drive that has proved insurmountable in her life and career. My mom is never my critic; she is only my biggest fan.

Beyond our own relationship, I now have a visual representation of a strong, tenacious, and godly woman who has approached all challenges with the question, "Why not?" She has proven the skills we have been given are not to be used just for one career, one job, or one trajectory... They are to be used to pursue all kinds of passions you have. From her example, don't ever paint yourself into a box. There is no box!

Back to what I said before, I come from a strong line of women in my family, women who passed down character traits of love, kindness, and resilience. I can't wait to start blazing my own trail as I start my life as a young professional. I have the examples from my family to follow. And if I am blessed to have a daughter someday, I hope to pass on that legacy as well.

Laura Lane Heathcott

July 2023

Introduction

"And the winner is… Kim Heathcott!" I slowly walked up to the Minneapolis convention center ballroom stage to accept the NAWBO National Women Business Owner of the Year award after hearing my name announced, a big smile on my face and my eyes rapidly blinking and unfocused. I was happy yet nervous to be standing in front of the crowd giving a speech that I'd just put together about five minutes earlier. I had not prepared any remarks. I would wing it like I did many things these days. There were three finalists who had been spotlighted that night from a month-long selection process, and my company, Clarion Security, had been picked as the winner. As my gaze panned from the back to the front to scan the vista on the walk, it all blurred together in a sea of dazzling festivity. Everyone was clapping and standing in their dressy cocktail attire as loud music blared from the stage, beckoning me toward the podium. Cheers from my friends and family at our table, waves of color washing over the packed ballroom from the elaborate stage set, a dome of light hovering over the podium on the 50-foot stage where I was about to literally have my shining moment…

It was all very glitzy and glamorous, which was so ironic because, after seven years of climbing to the pinnacle to claim this amazing national award, nothing about my journey there seemed glamorous at all. I was wearing a shiny cocktail dress, but I felt like I was covered in grime, dirt, sweat, and bruises from all the places I had been knocked down along the way.

There is nothing glamorous about the security guard industry. Movies tend to gloss perceptions of security guards in people's minds, but in reality it's a hard, tough business for the individuals who work in it and the people who run and own it. It takes a strong constitution, perseverance, and dedication to succeed. I didn't choose the industry; the industry chose me, which is often why an entrepreneur starts a business in the first place. Circumstances come together, which align a current opportunity with the entrepreneur skillset and some prior or current exposure to the industry. And I made sure to surround myself with top talent who did have prior exposure to the business since I did not. I had the basic skills in my backpack for potential success, plus an extra dose of stubbornness, which would come in handy every time I was on the verge of failure.

It all seems so exciting when you first start a company. Everything works really well on paper. You dream of all the money you will make quickly without much hardship along the way, setting out with everything you need in that fancy backpack with the wind at your back. That honeymoon period for me lasted about six months. That's when I started sliding down the mountain in my entrepreneurial journey to the top. It came from pressure from unrealistic expectations put on the company's performance, both from other people and myself.

It was if I would need to literally run up the mountain to make these goals:

- Achieving aggressive revenue goals in a tightly compressed amount of time.
- Creating a financially viable business with significant net income in the same period.
- Quickly breaking into the market as an unknown with stiff, well-established competition.

But unrealistic expectations + stubbornness = Kim resolves to achieve them at any cost. Even at much personal cost. So, when I ran up the mountain, inevitably I often slid down. Then I refocused and aimed for the top again as fast as I could, layered with a little more dirt and grime in the process but laser focused on getting further along each time.

Then there were the places where I fell down on the journey of my own accord from poor choices. It was easy to reel those off. Perfectionism and its toll on relationships and my own self-care, burnout and the impact on my health and interpersonal relationships... Those were bruises that took a long time to heal, not only for me but those who were caught up in the dysfunction.

As I energetically walked up in my finery to the lighted podium, it may have seemed so effortless to those looking on the outside in. "Look at all Kim accomplished in seven years!" "She has that many employees?" "She grew the company that quickly from a complete start-up?" "Kim scaled the business that fast and still took the time to give back and pour out her time and energy into helping other small business owners?"

How I saw it in that moment was different. Envision that shining podium as a sunlit mountaintop pinnacle—empty and waiting for someone to crest the last hill. Then, from the back of the mountain, up swings a pickaxe attached to a rope, slung to the top, landing solidly wedged on a rock. I slowly climb up the rope, almost unrecognizable from the hard journey up, sunburned and scarred. I trudge the last few steps bathed in light as the sun blazes away, baking the film of dirt into a hardened layer. I land right in the middle of the pinnacle with a giant smile on my face giving my identity away. I've changed on this journey. A lot.

And now, as I return to reality and I look around at the ballroom vista on every side, I'm drawn to my table and my people, those who gave me the support and encouragement I needed to make it to the top. And I remember you never achieve the greatest success on your own. And you certainly never want to be lonely at the top. Then I walked up to the lighted podium, shook the hands, accepted the award, took the requisite picture, and began my thank you speech.

According to the US Small Business Administration Office of Advocacy as written by Victoria Williams, "90 percent of all woman owned businesses had no employees" (2019). I had 450. That's a lot of responsibility and a whole lot of coordination and logistics. And an overwhelming ecosystem to protect clients' assets and people.

On paper, I really didn't look like a CEO who could achieve this kind of success, much less national acclaim and recognition. At the beginning of the business seven years earlier, I personally knew nothing about the security business. I knew nothing about running a company. I was a forty-seven-year-old stay-at-home mom who had "retired" from banking eight years prior in order to take care of my children.

So, then, how was I standing on that stage that day, winning a national award? I had built the first part of my career analyzing business financial performance, and I had a wealth of general knowledge about other people's businesses. Then I had fundamental leadership traits that are necessary for any entrepreneur: determination, hard work, drive, and resourcefulness. I surrounded myself with subject matter experts in sales and human resources who drove the one-two punch of growth in customers and employees. But the critical ingredient was found once I launched the business: passion. I didn't discover it until after the business was launched. It was the people, who ultimately grew in numbers to 450. That's what kept me motivated. Even those times when I failed my employees and, in turn, they failed me back.

I was scaling a mountain on my first try with no prior experience. And I picked a pinnacle to climb that was difficult and fraught with hardship along the way. And even though others can carry parts of the load, the responsibility rests on the CEO to take the company to the pinnacle. Many times, along the way, I was carrying nothing with me but my own stubborn independence and determination to keep moving up.

The beginning was a rough start to the journey. I really didn't want to start this company. It wasn't my idea. I had never managed an employee. I'm risk averse. This didn't fit me. I'm not the CEO type. I'm an introvert. Analytical, not creative. I was quiet, happy to watch others lead without putting myself at risk. But little by little, those first days turned into years, and I found my voice. I built my platform. I allowed myself to believe in my abilities. I listened to my employees and found compassion and empathy for their work. I became Ms. Kim. That suited me because I didn't want to be this CEO who was separated from my workers by my authority. The company became my passion. We were all in this together. Clarion could only succeed as my people had success. And now that I had developed that passion for my people and the business, I wanted to be their leader.

I wanted to motivate them with my leadership style that showed them I was not better than anyone else—a servant leader. We would all build this together. And so, we did—to tremendous success measured in achievements, awards, and acknowledgments.

Oh, I made mistakes. And lots of them. I lost good employees. I hired and kept plenty of bad ones. I took on too much responsibility and expected too much from others. I micro-managed some and gave too much latitude to others. I let the stress of pursuing excellence turn me brittle. I let my health deteriorate and lost work-life balance to work. But I never stopped caring, for my customers and my employees, for our value delivery and importance to clients. Saying goodbye less than three years later and walking away seemed inconceivable that NAWBO award night fresh off the high from such a significant award.

You have to be passionate, resourceful, and resilient if you choose to embark on an entrepreneurial journey, and the actual process of the journey may change how you define success when you reach the pinnacle. It certainly did for me.

My journey was hard. Yours is as well. Women, men, and minority small business owners; would-be entrepreneurs who dream of starting companies. Solopreneurs who want to grow and scale their business. Entrepreneurs that have "made it" on their journey but don't like the view from the pinnacle or what they see in their reflection: I have so many lessons I learned the hard way that I hope you don't have to repeat.

If just one of my stories can help or encourage you to keep moving forward to achieving success in your entrepreneurial journey, then my adventure with Clarion Security can mean so much more. If by reading this book, you alleviate just one problem, shift your attitude, cause a positive change, save a relationship, or get your business further along the journey, then that will be an amazing gift. I want to see you keep heading up your own mountain so you can let me know what you find once you get to the top.

PART 1

STARTING THE CLIMB

Barbie Dream House

Barbie: the staple of my childhood. She's really only five years older than I am. Now Barbie has a Facebook page where she is described as the following: "In 1959, Barbie launched as the original girl empowerment brand. From princess to president, astronaut to zoologist, there isn't a glass ceiling Barbie hasn't broken. Today, with over 200 careers and counting, she continues to show kids everywhere that you can be anything" (Barbie 2023).

Yet Barbie has never been a mom. She's a career girl and role model, independent and financially secure. Maybe that's why she can afford all those clothes and shoes and her very own Barbie Dream House.

For a long time, those were my aspirations as well: making a mark in my career, which started with getting a college education; going to a private, all-girls college-prep high school in Memphis, Tennessee… The question wasn't *if* you were going to college; it was *where*. I'm grateful for the mostly single-sex education and its impact on my formative years. We were encouraged to learn and lead in a focused, safe community amongst our peers.

And in college, I did. I landed at Vanderbilt University, and upon graduation I headed to Dallas, Texas, to start my career. I interviewed for positions and ended up with two simultaneous offers. One was in banking, and the other in real estate. Although I was interested in the real estate position, my thoughts were that working my way up the corporate ladder would be tough, as the position seemed more administrative. Both banking and real estate in the '80s were male-dominated at the higher levels, and I didn't want to pigeonhole myself and get stuck in a support role. Not that the banking offer was much better. They both paid $18,000 a year, and the bank job was as an operations officer trainee. What that really meant was that for the next year, I would work in areas of the bank where someone was on vacation or they had an empty slot, opening a bank account, working as a teller, answering calls in customer service, and working in the proof department. I really hope a computer does this proof job now, but what I did back then was look at signature cards and verify every cleared check from the night before to make sure the signatures matched. Like, all day long.

I don't think Barbie could handle that job, but that position taught me a few things. If you do a really good job in whatever you are doing, you will catch the attention of supervisors and managers. And attitude is everything. I never complained one minute about what they asked me to do. I was there every day, giving it my best. Well, maybe not on those mornings when I had been out soaking in the single Dallas life the night before. But those jobs were pretty forgiving, and I seemed to rally through. And the final lesson is that, in a career trajectory, there comes a time when you have to be courageous about the next step up. For me, it was exactly one year later, when I went to the operations manager of the bank and asked how I could be a loan officer. It took a lot to muster up my courage to ask at twenty-two years old, but I knew I couldn't get stuck in my current position for much longer.

This was the late '80s, and lending in Texas had ground to a halt due to the savings and loan crisis and the spillover effect on general banking. Thankfully, he didn't shut down the conversation. He told me I would need to move to another city where they were headquartered and live for three months to go to credit school. I don't think he thought I would take him up on it, but I did. And that's what started my long-term career in banking and finance.

2002

"The flight is canceled. Can you come pick me up?" I asked my husband. It was the last flight to Atlanta out of Memphis for the night. It was a relief to be headed back home. My two-year-old daughter had a meltdown at the airport a few hours earlier. I hadn't traveled for work since she was born, so she couldn't understand why I would leave her. And I was wondering that myself. Emotions were running high with everyone in the family who felt this conflict between career and motherhood. Until four years earlier, I was 100 percent career. I was driven and focused on moving up the corporate ladder in the financial world. That is until 1998. I was thirty-three years old when I had my first child, so when he was born, I had a full-blown career that I enjoyed and thrived in.

I seemed to manage the fine line between work and home until my daughter was born. Then there was one career, but two young children pulling at my heartstrings. I had choices to make. And they were made quickly. I never flew to Atlanta. I threw out my business cards with "Vice President" on them and shifted to "Stay-at-Home Mom." The career I thought was so important to me evaporated, and I never regretted it. My priority was my family, and staying home with my children became my focus. My new circle of friends never knew my professional history. It didn't matter. I had retired, or so I thought—until I was called out of retirement and drafted into starting a business.

THE ONE QUESTION
When you start to achieve critical milestones in your business, it often leads to media opportunities and interviews. Whether it was a TV, magazine, or in-person interview, I wouldn't always know every question, but I would anticipate the one that was always asked:

"Kim, why did you decide to start a security guard company?"

I didn't bristle or bite back because if I were in their position, I would be asking the same thing. This introverted, sheltered, reserved woman who, before starting her company, was spending her time leading bible studies, volunteering as swim team mom, and carpooling her kids to sleepovers and school, was now leading 450 security guards in protecting millions of dollars of property and lives of people day in and day out. And a fourth of the guards were armed guards carrying pistols. How did this former soccer mom know the ins and outs of a Sig Sauer P226? Of all the businesses Kim could start, that was the one she picked? And I laugh with them. Because it makes no sense. I get it. A mom who left behind a banking career in 2002 in order to stay at home with her young children running a business that was typically run by men with a military and law enforcement background with years of experience?

"Kim, why did you decide to start a security guard company?" What I really just want to say is, "I don't know. I didn't know anything about the security guard business and wouldn't of my own accord. My husband did." It was his passion. He had built another business in the industry and grown it with his salesmanship but had left that business, not over business matters but rather due to personal issues. I wish I could have hit fast forward a few years and remembered that, even with tremendous financial success, when you lose sight of the personal dynamics, it may have consequences that impact far more than the business.

But I wasn't thinking that deep or even past the moment at hand. We started the company in the midst of a difficult financial season. I really didn't want to go back to work. I was comfortable in my life and routines raising my children. But that's the way life works. When you are presented with hard choices to make, the best options are to pick from the cards dealt before you. As much as I would have liked to throw every single one of those cards back on the discard pile, unfortunately, there was nothing else any better to pick up. I had been out of the job market for too long. We needed a bigger win than I could get from a return to banking.

"Kim, why did you decide to start a security guard company?" And finally, I started to answer in a tongue-in-cheek fashion, "My husband was such a good salesman that he convinced me I could run a business in an industry I knew nothing about with no business network and no experience running any type of business." Which, though said in jest, was actually the truth. Whether he truly believed I could be successful, the more critical issue was that I really didn't. And that was how I became an entrepreneur at forty-seven years old. It would take me a little longer to discover the why, and a long time later to discover the "why me." Why would I start a security guard company?

According to Elizabeth McBride, the average age of the founders of the highest-growth startups was forty-five. Her hypothesis is, "Given that caring for children generally causes women, on average, to lag a few years in their careers, I think it's a safe bet that more older women are starting successful companies than in the past, and that they account for a growing share of the top startups" (McBride 2019).

For a long time, I grieved over that gap in my work résumé. But I realize now that sometimes a gap causes you to propel yourself into your own business to make up for lost time on the career and earnings path. And I love the fact I can be a role model for women who really want to stay at home with their children but also worry they've tanked their careers. You truly cannot have it all at the same time. But you can stop and start to prioritize your goals based on current circumstances. So, Elizabeth, yes and yes. You can have gaps in your career that are filled with family priorities and reinvent your professional career a multitude of times over, which could also include starting a successful business later in life.

The original question was asked and answered. I started the company. Though it wasn't my initial decision, once it was made, I owned it. Literally and figuratively. And that meant clarifying the roles. I didn't want the company to be seen as a sham cover and just be a figurehead for my husband, especially since he was the one who had the background in the business and had made his prior company a great success. He had faith in my ability to run the company. And I would prove it out. So, the first item on my agenda was to ensure I would comply with all certifications as a women-owned business and draft operating documents that gave me 100 percent control over everything in the company. Contracts, banking, personnel—I never wanted there to be an integrity issue from certifying agencies, customers, or other women-owned businesses, and that is what motivated me to be completely above board in this aspect. Through the years, I blazed a trail for women-owned and controlled businesses, knowing that both on paper and in actual operation, that was exactly what Clarion Security was. I never dreamed that decision would impact me personally and have painful consequences just eight years later.

APRIL 2010

"Barbie, watch out. I'm going to try out this CEO/business owner gig and see how I do there." Key word "try."

It was time to set up my pretend company. That's how it felt to me early on. I would do things I liked and found fun in those early days. Name, colors, logo, office space. It was like building a house and designing the floor plan, picking paint colors, and dreaming about the design and feel. Much more fun than the nuts and bolts of construction and the hard day-to-day tasks of building step by step. Same for my company. This was my dream/design phase. Who wanted to think about how to actually run the business? I didn't really, not at first. Coming up with a name was much more exciting. I wanted it to mean something significant.

As I spent one night scrolling through old English shields on the internet, I found one with a unique orange feature—a clarion. *Clarion* means a call to battle, even a euphemism for good against evil. For a security company, that seemed spot on. And no one had claimed Clarion in the security world, so it was perfect. The orange Clarion on the shield then translated easily into deciding my color scheme: orange and charcoal gray. Check check. Barbie's dream-house-turned-security-dream-company was moving right along.

Next, I needed a logo. I found a freelance team that designed some potential logos. Again, I wanted the logo to be purposeful and meaningful. We reviewed their designs, and one was a double shield. The simplicity appealed to me, and I saw the potential in the design. The shields symbolized protection. One of the shields would symbolize the customers, and the other would symbolize the employees. Ultimately, my mantra became, "Protecting clients. Valuing employees." At some point, when my company became missional for me, the logo took on a great significance, but for now I was just thrilled about how great the patch looked on the charcoal gray security shirt.

Then it was time to actually find a location for the Clarion dream house. We had to have a physical office location with its own bathroom to do drug testing. But I was adamant about not paying premium pricing and getting a lease with a one year out, showing my skepticism about making this a real go. All I was thinking about was how to abandon the effort in short order without having to be on the hook for an expensive lease if we couldn't get the company off the ground. Clearly not the right attitude. Perhaps I thought this whole concept could somehow just go away, and we would find some other way to earn a living. But I was playing along for now. And I found just the right spot. Conveniently located less than a mile from my home, it was a Class B walk-up property in the heart of town, with one bathroom, a tiny conference room, one interior office, and a bullpen space in the back with no windows. Nothing about this place was dreamy. But it was geographically convenient, had a bathroom, came with preexisting ugly cubicles in the back, and was not very expensive.

I took the biggest cubicle in the back dungeon and gave the office to my human resources manager so she would have a bird's eye view of the bathroom to make sure there wouldn't be a rash of fake drug tests. That's what she told me anyway. I was so naive. There would be so much more than faked drug tests that I would have to deal with in this business. But for now, perfect! We bought some used furniture on Craigslist to round out our furnishings, and voilà—instant office.

Now we had uniforms, a functional office, and an HR manager. We then found an operations manager and hired a sales assistant. Now, lest I forget to illustrate, Clarion Security had no customers or actual security guards. Remember, this was the fun, faux stage of running a company without the pressure of performing for clients. Ah, wouldn't it be so wonderful if you could just suspend reality right there and live in that fantasy forever? We had money in the bank to cover operating expenses and salaries, and we were working on the revenue part.

Now it was time to play at the Clarion dream house. I would take my kids to school, go to my "office," dabble in some of the business infrastructure, then head to the carpool line. It was a low-commitment, low-stress environment—and a complete denial of reality. But at that time, this wasn't my house or my dream. I played along for a few months. Until we actually landed our first customers, that is. Then the reality came crashing in, and a few months later, the implications of what we had started became a sobering wake-up call.

And with that, I packed my Clarion dream house into a nice starter backpack, ready for the climb. It was time to start in earnest. Nowhere to go but up.

See you, Barbie. This is getting real. Time to be an actual CEO now.

Client Problems

"Kim, the board of directors have voted to make a change in security providers." Her voice was measured with a low tone meant to convey some type of care and concern. The property manager slowly voiced the sentence, which was probably rehearsed a time or two before calling. "I'm sorry to tell you that the board has voted to bring in a new security provider." It had been a tortuous process getting to this call. Interviews, problem-solving, politicking. The vote was in, and we were out. She was the designated messenger delivering the bad news. "When?" I asked in a flat voice. That was my only question. "Okay. Thanks," I responded back to her in an equally measured tone. Then I hung up the phone, dejectedly staring out the window. I thought this might happen, but it was a gut punch to hear.

It had started a few months ago with a few security incidents in the back of the neighborhood, this beautiful gated development that had not had a single security incident in the seven years we had provided the security. We had been hired to manage access control at the front gate, which had been performing well. The criminals in the back took advantage of darkness, strategic positioning out of camera sight, and the comfort level of residents who lived in a gated community.

It seemed so unfair. I wanted to say, "Do you know I've personally covered the gate several times when my guard didn't show up? I'm the owner who constantly checks and coaches the guards here day in and day out! I handle issues no one even knows about. Seven years without issue!" Then I justified our position to myself as I got more agitated, "Doesn't that goodwill count for anything?" But it was too late. The neighbors were upset, the board needed to take action, and the solution was to make a change in guard service regardless of how well we had performed until this unfortunate situation.

As I looked out at the quiet, lovely neighborhood, the tears slowly rolled down my cheeks. This one hurt on so many levels. This was both business and personal. It had been our first account. The customer who took a chance on us in the very beginning. The one that turned the dream house into the real house. A neighborhood community that chose to believe in our team and our promise to protect. The one I put my heart into. The one that believed in us. The one we swore we would not let down—until, in their eyes, we did. And, as I bitterly took in the news, perception felt like reality. This was not by a stretch my biggest customer. But in my mind, it had always personally been my most important one. Lost.

RISK: THE POSSIBILITY OF SOMETHING BAD HAPPENING

Security is a tricky business. It's generally outsourced by companies who want the protection that security provides without the liability and risk associated with the position. So that means the third-party security provider takes the risk and responsibility if there is a security breach and is paid to protect the client's assets and property. It's a pretty tall order accepting 100 percent of the risk for any incidents. That by itself might seem daunting. Now, combine that with criminals who are crafty and sneaky and could potentially disguise themselves as employees, or those who could just be common criminals constantly watching a property for vulnerability and opportunity.

Not only that, but security guards are often hired to screen visitors at gates, greet customers and clients with a warm, pleasant personality, and check clients' properties to ensure there are no water leaks or other property damage on the premises. Oh, and be ready to manage a dispute, de-escalate a tense situation, and step up to a leadership role in a crisis. Wow. So not only were my guards expected to exhibit superior customer service, but they also needed to watch over properties with care, be on the constant lookout for criminal activity, and do whatever they could to deter any thefts. This was intense and real. My clients had high expectations of guard performance, which was most often tested in a crisis.

Our first customers were a combination of many of the different types of security guard functions. A security sampler, if you will. Gate access control, overnight exterior golf cart parking lot patrols, and after-hour building patrols. Each of these had its own nuances and challenges. I was learning on the job, and it was fascinating.

As I focused on providing great customer service to our clients, I measured my success in client complaints. There were five categories I targeted to minimize complaints, things I worked really hard on *trying* to control that I thought were key drivers to client satisfaction.

1. PREVENTIVE DECISIONS

There were instances with new clients when I saw issues that could lead to problems. And the last thing I wanted was for a problem to develop. I was new to security but well-versed in how temptations could lead to a bad decision. Crime is often a combination of opportunity and access. For instance, on our first day in an office building we took on as a client, I found out there was a master key on the guard keyring that opened up hundreds of office suites. It required rekeying the building but shutting down both opportunity and access. We needed to get into the building. But a guard would never need access into a private office suite. I didn't have years of experience in the industry, but I could bring detailed observation skills and common sense. That was very much in my control. It started to get harder after that.

2. MANAGING EXPECTATIONS

This seemed to be so straightforward, but access control illustrated the conflicting experience of doing the job the right way offset by the frustrations of those inconvenienced. It was the same problem, just a different client. It could be someone laying on the horn in a line of vehicles waiting to enter an office building complex held up by someone missing a badge, a backup of eighteen-wheelers spilling back out onto the highway waiting to drop their load held up at the gate by a driver with paperwork not matching the system. A long line of employees waiting to be scanned by a metal detector wand when exiting off their shift who needed to show everything in their lunch boxes and were searched underneath their jackets to ensure they weren't walking out of the warehouse with any product. The pressure to perform the task accurately, consistently, and diligently. And complaints sure to follow if speed and accuracy were not both followed.

My stance was for our employees to do the job the right way. There may be complaints, but they wouldn't be from the customer. And the clients seemed to appreciate our company being a stickler for following their rules and driving that home to our security staff. However, it got progressively difficult with the more diverse client base we were growing and the larger number of employees we kept adding. How could I best convey to our staff exactly what the customer wanted? What were the best ways to instruct my guards? I spent the better part of the next few years brainstorming about the best way to teach.

3. PRACTICAL COMMON-SENSE JOB AIDS

This was the hardest task I worked on, one for which I never came up with a magical formula. The majority of people learn by a visual learning style, as opposed to reading or listening to someone teach them how to do the job. They need to be actively learning. According to Tom Alexander, "People retain 80 percent of what they see, compared to 20 percent of what they read and only 10 percent of what they hear" (2018). We would spend hours writing down detailed instructions on the nuances of each post. Creating quizzes. Laminated job aids. "Post orders" that could be up to fifty pages long for a complicated truck gate at a distribution warehouse. I put together instructional videos. There was no way a new guard was going to catch on the first time because, by the law of averages, the majority needed to see the process in action. This works amazingly well when you have a consistent team in place. The moment there was a new or replacement guard, it would be bumpy. "Kim, there's a new guard here who doesn't know what they are doing." And my client was right. What could I do to prevent the issues? I couldn't prevent all of them, but I had an answer to many of them, and it was...

ACTIVE MANAGEMENT

Early on, I found the secret ingredient to managing new and inexperienced guards, replacement guards, late guards, and absentee guards. They were precious cargo driving around in my silver Prius vehicles all over the city. My experienced site supervisors, patrol supervisors, and operations managers. Supervisors who knew the complicated posts and could go train a new guard or fill in if needed. These officers fanned out over the city, and I could count on them to handle the issues, night and day, and especially on the weekends. We also had post commanders who would manage a large client with multiple locations and a large group of employees who might have to be on one of the sites at 2:00 a.m., if needed. I didn't appreciate what I had at the time or the devotion most of them showed to our company. I lost some, and their absence would be devastating until the right replacement came along. Looking back now, I wish I had paid them more and verbally thanked them privately and publicly often. Instead, I spent a good amount of time trying to influence them with my thoughts and ideas.

DRIVING ACCOUNTABILITY

I had the same lecture I gave year after year to my supervisors. The ones who had heard it before just sat there and rolled their eyes as I launched into it again. "Everyone, let me illustrate," I said excitedly to the audience around the table at my weekly supervisor meeting. "You are running late. You are in Downtown Memphis, and you drive down the main road, Poplar Avenue, to get to a site in the suburb just to the east of the city in Germantown. You speed down Poplar, twenty miles over the speed limit, because you know you won't be stopped. Ten feet into Germantown, your car slows down to five miles or less over the speed limit. Why? Because you will be getting a speeding ticket within five minutes." Accountability and oversight. I went on to put an exclamation point on my speech. "You are the same person who just drove from one place to another. The only variable that changed was that there was a consequence to your actions." And my speech was over. The more we provided oversight to the posts, the better our performance would be.

Yet that was where I had the push/pull that was the most difficult to manage. I had a scarcity of resources. I could have a patrol supervisor going to visit posts that was needed to train a new guard. And to be done right, that would take a big chunk of time. They were both important. If I picked covering an open post, I just had to have faith in my people doing the right thing the majority of the time on each of the posts. But again, that's where things got tricky. Because in spite of my best efforts, these things I could not control:

- Employees with their own agendas, which were not in the best interest of the company; and
- Criminals

RESPONSE: A REPLY OR REACTION

Crisis. Something happened. Maybe it wasn't even a crime. It could have been a traffic accident with injuries on the property. A truck that had run into the guardhouse, knocking down the steps. An office building that lost power and tenants stuck in the elevator. Lots of things happen on properties after hours.

Criminal activity happened. A vehicle break-in. Theft. Armed robbery. Trespassing. Police vehicles on the scene.

What would be worse than any of these scenarios? It would be having these events happening on our watch that we didn't report to the customer. We might not have been able to control or deter all the criminal activity. But at the minimum, it was imperative that we let the client know, preferably in real time.

Transparency and open communication were critical to client satisfaction. Where it got difficult was when emotion got involved. This is where I realized I couldn't manage some customer expectations. Security is a big expense. And when there are incidents, it's human nature to assign blame. For example, a customer at a retail shopping center leaves a computer in the backseat of their car and money in the console. The security guard passes by in a vehicle. The criminal scout alerts his partner, who punches out the lock and takes the computer but leaves the money because he's found a gun in the glove compartment, all in about a minute or less before the guard rotates back. Who's to blame? The customer for leaving valuables in the car? The criminal? More often than not, if it happens more than once, the security guard company is the culprit. The guard company was hired to deter crime and failed, regardless of the reasons. And I understand it could be the security guard who didn't do their job properly. But there was immense pressure to perform in the face of a constant criminal presence.

From the outset, I felt like I could handle the customer service part of the business. However, I was incredibly naive when it came to the criminal side of the business. I didn't understand the level of sophistication of criminals, and we would be tested constantly over the years. It became the major crux of stress in my role as CEO. My desperate need to prove to our clients that we could provide superior customer service, all the while fighting against the criminals who were determined to undermine our performance at every step. My natural personality is a problem solver, which is suited well to managing company performance. But when year after year of difficult situations and a never-ending stream of problems piled on, I started drowning in the stress of managing through the hard situations. I didn't have the wherewithal to understand my psyche and what was being triggered by these big issues. I knew enough to realize the bigger we grew, the less I was able to control. Still, I stubbornly continued to try my best.

That's when I started becoming more anxious. The more accounts we won, the more issues arose. And I started to take it personally. I felt like I was letting my clients down. Even though there were elements clearly out of my control, it still made me sick every time we got a call that something had happened on Clarion's watch. And then there was the underlying fear. We were the new kid in town, the brand-new company that needed to get it right most all the time. I was afraid if we didn't, we would lose customers, and our family would suffer financially.

So that afternoon, when I got the cancellation notice, I was sick and sad. With some perspective much later, I understood there were more issues at play in that decision to switch security providers, and the security incident provided a reason for them to make a change. We delivered a great product for what we were hired to do. That account launched us into the market. We were given a chance and capitalized on it a thousand times over. There were some things I could control and some I had to let go of.

Risk: The possibility of something bad happening. And in this incident, something bad did happen. But could I frame it a different way by reflecting on the positive?

Reward: Something good had already happened. This client had launched our business, and seven years later we had a vast array of customers, great reputation, and thriving business. We could lose this one. It would be OK.

In business, you will lose customers. It's part of the business cycle, and it's important to take the emotion out of it. Ask yourself what you could have done better. Every loss is an opportunity to evaluate what got to the point of a customer leaving. Even more important is letting a customer go graciously. And after some time has passed, ask the customer what you could have done better. You never know when handling the situation in a humble way may provide an opportunity to win that client back in the future. Never burn the bridge, no matter how you feel about the loss. Always remember it's business, not personal. It's okay to shed the tears. Sit in that feeling for a moment, but then brush it off and keep going up.

People Matter

"Who's more important, the customer or the employee?" It was an impromptu question my operations manager would ask at the new hire orientation. You could see the confused look on the faces of the new hires. They didn't want to be put on the spot and answer wrong. And it seemed like a trick question. "Ummm, the customer? Isn't the customer always supposed to be the most important?" was the usual answer they would give. He would give a long theatrical pause and then say, "It's the employees!" in his deep booming voice, preaching to the confused room. His rationale followed. "You take care of the employees, and they will take care of the customers."

But would they? Could we really motivate that type of altruistic behavior by our employees? And if the employee was more important than the customer, did that mean we valued employees more than customers? How could we succeed if we weren't focused on driving performance on behalf of our clients?

He didn't ask for my answer. And from my perspective, it wasn't a choice between the two. The two were intertwined. I wouldn't have a viable business without customers. But I couldn't perform a service for the clients without the people. My people were my product. At that very moment, someone wasn't determining how good a company we were by my management skills. They were making an assessment based on the guard standing outside the door they had just walked out of. Or the one who just signed them in. Or the one patrolling the parking lot where they shopped. An assessment made in a few seconds' time based on their perception and interaction with just that one security guard.

My people mattered. That was fundamental, and I knew it. And it was my job to lay the groundwork from day one to make them feel as if they did. And I didn't have a clue where to start.

I had never been a manager of people before. My banking career mainly consisted of project work, spreadsheets, and analyzing financial plans. I was really good at managing myself and working on the computer. In all of my various positions, I never once managed a single person.

The first part of building the business appealed to my natural skill set. Researching how to get the proper licenses. Creating a website. Building the operational systems. Putting into place payroll, scheduling, and financial systems. All the details needed to function properly as a business.

"What do I do about the people?" I asked myself in a bit of a panic. I was woefully inadequate in that arena. I needed some help.

MY FIRST HIRE

It had to start at the very top, a human resources manager who had the experience and could build the infrastructure for our growth. And I hit the jackpot on my first try even before we opened our doors. Renette would become the backbone of Clarion Security. She had steely determination, emphatic conviction, strong experience, intelligence, and loyalty—that is a rare find. And she was a good foil for me because, at first, I tended to be a softie and a little bit of a pushover when it came to conflict and hard personnel decisions. With an utter commitment to our mission, I would trust her implicitly in the years to come. So many times throughout those ten years, when I didn't think I could make it another day with the stress, drama, and personnel and customer issues, I knew I could count on Renette to keep things together. It was an amazing partnership. Because at both of our cores, she believed in me, and I counted on her. We knew we were brought together by divine appointment, and we took that bond seriously.

Renette was more like a business partner than an employee. She taught me the rules and the ropes and kept our company intact with sound policies and procedures. And she would challenge me when she disagreed. But it was my interaction with some of our first employees that completely changed my perspective and caused me to finally engage in this venture with my whole heart.

MY FIRST EMPLOYEES

When we were scrambling for those first few accounts in the first year of the business's existence, we had to come up with a competitive edge. And the first obvious one was the matter of price. My bill rate corresponded to my labor rate. It was a simple ratio. But in order to price at or slightly below the competition, the first bill rates keyed off of pay rates that were low. And it was nowhere near a living wage, which the Global Coalition Living Wage describes as "the minimum wage required to afford a decent standard of living which includes food, water, housing, education, health care, transportation, clothing, and other essential needs" (2018). Some of my primary competitors even paid minimum wage, although they offered sixty-hour workweeks. How would we attract quality workers at such a low rate? On paper, those pay rates seemed so harsh, pay rates below poverty level for a security officer who was expected to protect millions in property. But how else could we win business when the customers would get up to five proposals and take the lowest bid? The bid rate was a proportionate increase directly on the pay rate. If I wanted to win a contract, the math was simple: keep my pay rate low, manage my profit margins tight, keep operating expenses skinny, and offer a bid rate that was better than my competition.

That was our initial strategy—but we had a people problem because of it: No one wanted to come work for us. We were an unknown upstart in a city with entrenched significant competition, paying pretty much the same as all the other competitors. I fretted over how we could move forward. What good would it be to win a big contract when we couldn't staff it? Still in our infancy, I wondered, Why would a guard jump ship from their current employer to work for us? What compelling reason was out there that I hadn't thought about?

THE BREAKTHROUGH

About six months after we won our first few contracts, a tall African American man with a big smile and imposing presence walked into the office to fill out an application. He was wearing a security uniform from an established competitor. Our industry was known for employees who jumped from one security guard company to another. There wasn't much loyalty. And I was starting to figure out why. To gain loyalty, you had to feel like more than a hired mercenary (make that a hired, very low-compensated mercenary). Learning of his story and why he chose to walk through our doors that day gave me an epiphany that shifted the whole approach I chose to take with my employees.

"What brought you to our office to apply?" Renette asked him. I could tell she was surprised a security guard with this much presence and experience had walked into our little office, knowing we had only a few tiny customers and little to no brand recognition in the Memphis market. "Why Clarion?" I was curious as well. I was sitting in the back of the office, out of sight, but I could hear the conversation.

He responded, "Last Saturday, my oldest daughter got married. I hadn't taken a day off in six months, and I had told my company well in advance I needed to be off on Saturday to walk her down the aisle. On Friday night at 8:00 p.m., another guard 'called off' his shift for the weekend. My supervisor told me there was no one else who could work. I had to come in or be fired."

I couldn't resist jumping into the conversation, so I rushed up to the front. "How could they give you an ultimatum like that? It was your daughter's wedding! There was no one else who could work the shift?" The words came tumbling out of my mouth, responding to the injustice and inhumanity of it all.

He answered, "I guess not, but I wasn't going to miss my daughter's wedding. So, they fired me, and here I am."

I left Renette there to handle the paperwork as I walked to the back, processing that conversation. Their loss was our gain. But his words kept resonating in my mind. Over and over I thought, *That's no way to treat your employees.* It's bad enough that security officers weren't getting paid fairly for what they were worth and the work they were doing, but to treat people like a cog in a wheel with no compassion for their personal lives... I knew covering posts was the top priority of any guard company, but there *had* to be another way to make that happen.

And in that moment, I made a vow to myself. I would do everything I could possibly do to run a professionally staffed operation, but I would choose not to do it at the disadvantage of my people. We all have family, health situations, car problems, and conflicts that will collide in some way with work. Maybe that was a female perspective that didn't permeate the typical male-dominated, militaristic-type security guard companies, but my moral convictions were only giving me this option. I would offer a different approach.

Our company needed to connect with our guards in tangible, specific ways that would convey empathy and compassion. If we showed we cared about our employees with our policies and procedures, then and only then could I hope they would care about our mission to protect our client's assets and people. I put together a master plan of perks, incentives, honors, gifts, and policies that were different from any of the competition. And it worked. We were able to grow immensely fast and staff the ever-growing customer list. Ten years later, at 450 employees, we were the largest woman-owned business in the city of Memphis.

In those same ten years, I learned many lessons from being in the "people" business:

- Even if a business idea is not yours, make it your own by putting your passion into execution.

Being inexperienced in an industry can bring a fresh approach to how you run the business. You can be creative in your decisions and policies and not do things because "that's the way they are always done in this business." After I had the moment with the fired guard that day, I began to implement policies based on my personal convictions that a typical security guard operator would never do. Those policies worked for our company and aligned values of empathy and compassion with our operational procedures. Could we have been successful had we been more typical of our competitors? Maybe. But it wouldn't have been authentic to my leadership style. And it wouldn't have defined the culture we established.

- A business based on people who are the product must establish a clear culture that engages and motivates the employees.

"Corporate culture matters. How management chooses to treat its people impacts everything—for better or for worse" (Guy 2021). What culture did we create? #ClarionCares. Valuing employees. Protecting clients. It permeated throughout the company. We were different. And we started attracting employees from competitors who were tired of being treated like a commodity. It's not easy to get to and keep an employee base of 450 who work in one of the most stressful jobs in the country.

Was my operations manager right, after all? His theory was, "You take care of the employees, and they will take care of the customers." My spin would be, "You show your employees by action and behavior that you care for them. They feel respected by the company as valued contributors. Then they take pride in the company whose brand they represent. The hoped-for outcome would be for them to stay longer and do their job with professionalism." Maybe that's saying the exact same thing. This leads me to my next lesson:

- Round out your top team with people with complementary strengths to position for success.

For the ten years I ran my company, Renette ran the whole people operation. She did a great job of bringing me into issues where I needed to get involved, but other than that, she ran the HR machine day in and day out. It was her own mini-operation within our company, and I was good with it. Because as I will illustrate in future chapters, I still had a lot of mistakes I would make and a lot to learn in the people department.

However, I never meshed well with my highly intelligent, very experienced, formidable operations manager. We were oil and water. An army veteran and retired military police officer, he ran the operations well and brought a wealth of experience to my operational staff that I just didn't have in the business. My perception was that he thought he could probably run the company better with his résumé than mine. And I was determined to prove him wrong. A bit of a power struggle but illustrative of the fact that you don't have to be completely aligned with your top team to be successful. He got along incredibly well with everyone else in the top management team and brought credibility and experience to the large significant accounts we were about to win. Looking back, I could have lost some of that chip on my shoulder where he was concerned. But in the moment, he felt too entrenched in the old guard company ways, and I was blazing my trail *my* way.

With my husband handling the sales side of the business excellently, we had a highly functioning team put together, ready to navigate our way to the top. We were together pushing our way up to new heights. It was when the pace picked up that some began to falter. That was a lesson I would learn much later on as I led the big push to go higher and faster than some of the team could keep up. But for now, we were amazingly better together.

Servant Leadership

Whoever is kind to the poor lends to the LORD, and he will reward them for what they have done. (Proverbs 19:17, NIV)

"Ms. Kim, I really need to cut back my hours." I looked at her in surprise, wondering why she would request a cut in a forty-hour shift. She had worked several different shifts for me over the past two years. Starting overnight so she could get her kids to school in the morning, then second shift because some family was helping out. "But I just gave you a first shift!" I pushed back. It was one that all my single mothers wanted: A weekday forty-hour shift starting each day at 6:00 a.m.; a shift that worked around the elementary school schedule and would eliminate paying babysitters. I had learned that much in my short time managing this business.

She elaborated, "If I cut my hours to twenty-four hours per week, I can get government assistance from subsidized housing and food stamps." At first, I was taken aback by her request. It didn't jive with my value system for appropriate work ethic. Then I put myself in her shoes. At her pay rate, she couldn't take care of her family. Even at forty hours, it wasn't above federal standards for poverty level. So rather than have to work two jobs and not be there for her children, was it better to let her qualify for care to get some assistance?

LEADERSHIP STYLES

Leaders generally lead with one pre-eminent leadership style, which is often based on their personality, skills, values, and experiences. According to the International Institute for Management Development, there are six primary leadership styles.

1. "Transformational Leadership—A leadership style that emphasizes change and transformation and inspires followers.
2. "Delegative Leadership—A hands-off leader which delegates initiative to team members.
3. "Authoritative Leadership—Visionary leaders who chart a course and encourage others to follow.
4. "Transaction (Managerial) Leadership—A give-and-take style that emphasizes structure and relies on rewards and punishments.
5. "Participative Leadership—Leaders who listen to their employees and involve them in the decision-making process.
6. "Servant Leadership—Ethical decision making that puts the needs of others first" (2023).

SERVANT LEADERSHIP

This leadership style gained popularity after being discussed in an essay published by Robert Greenleaf, titled "The Servant as Leader" (2015). The concept is leading with humility and selflessness rather than domination or power; and putting the needs of others at the forefront.

It wasn't difficult to discern my style. "Servant leader" fit right down the line with my value system and personality. And it was a radical departure from the typical command and control hierarchies of guard companies.

I had heard stories from employees who were not treated with respect by other companies. And I vowed to be a compassionate employer of choice. Those values would be rolled out with policies that backed them up. The reality of my employees' plight was quite evident. My people were poor, and many were suffering because of it. It was systemic, and my business wasn't going to get them out of that situation. But I could make decisions that could help them in their plight.

WORKING POOR STATISTICS

Seven million individuals were among the "working poor" in 2018 when we hit our high employee count of 450, according to data from the Bureau of Labor Statistics (2020). Among the highlights of the research:

- "Women were more likely than men to be among the working poor (5.3 percent and 3.7 percent, respectively). In addition, Blacks or African Americans and Hispanics or Latinos continued to be much more likely than Whites and Asians to be among the working poor.
- Individuals who were employed in service occupations continued to be more likely to be among the working

poor than those employed in other major occupational groups.
- Among families with at least one member in the labor force for twenty-seven weeks or more, those with children under eighteen years old were over five times as likely as those without children to live in poverty. Families maintained by women were more than twice as likely as families maintained by men to be living below the poverty level" (2020).

Given these statistics, my officers had so many burdens stacked against them. The majority of my workforce was African-American. Many of my employees were single mothers, with none of them making a living wage. My employee base was filled with the working poor.

Amy Glasmeier, now a professor of economic geography and regional planning at the Massachusetts Institute of Technology, developed the Living Wage Calculator. As she indicates, "This tool uses more specific data to gauge the basic needs of American families. It estimates the cost of food, child care, health care (both insurance premiums and typical health care costs), housing, transportation and other necessities" (2023).

"The living wage is the minimum income standard that, if met, draws a very fine line between the financial independence of the working poor and the need to seek out public assistance or suffer consistent and severe housing and food insecurity. In light of this fact, the living wage is perhaps better defined as a minimum subsistence wage for persons living in the United States" (Glasmeier 2023).

Our wages were never going to provide our employees with the ability to hit the living wage mark. Our employees would either have to get federal assistance, or find additional sources of income, or live without basic essentials such as healthcare. Quickly, I was learning how hard it was for my employees. And although my heart was breaking in many ways, it just made me understand I couldn't solve these bigger issues. I could only manage what I could control. I could make decisions and policies that could support my people. And that became my new mission.

ACTION PLANS

It was not lost on me that, with 95 percent of my employees being African American, I had the opportunity to learn and be empathetic to their world. And perhaps on my end, I could offer my employees a model for a servant leader who could exhibit a humble attitude. That was my goal and objective from the beginning. I think that's why it didn't bother me when I had to stand a post every now and then in the early years. I was grateful I could set the example I wasn't above a single employee, and I would (and did) walk a mile in their shoes.

That day talking with that single mother was one example of how my eyes were opened, and it challenged me to how I could be a more compassionate leader understanding more of the many difficulties my employees faced. This was my company and my new mission field. There were decisions and policies I could choose that could impact their lives in a more positive manner. And I was very grateful for that. My answer to the single mother was quick. "I'll cut your shift to twenty-four hours a week." Because I could and I wanted to do it. As hard as it was so many days in the world of running this security business, my employees had it harder.

Over the years, I did as much as I could to be a compassionate employer with both big and small policies. There are, however, downfalls to this leadership style. And I experienced these consequences to varying degrees of seriousness. According to the Institute for Management Development, these were some of top concerns:

"Not prioritizing bottom-line results: The juxtaposition between sacrificing results to ensure happiness which leads to not being demanding enough from a performance level" (2023).

I struggled mightily with this. I didn't set clear standards for performance as I should have. And there were times when employees took advantage of my softness, and I let them off the hook. Had I held them accountable they may not have made it, but it could also have pushed them to perform at a higher level and benefit the whole organization.

"Difficulty connecting with leaders" (2023):

This was an unusual leadership style for the guard business. And some of my top managers who came from distinctly opposite management had difficulty relating. I am sure that contributed to the difficulty I faced connecting with those operations managers.

"**Difficulty in Scaling:** This leadership style works best in smaller companies" (2023).

That's why when we grew so fast, I put so much pressure on my supervisors. I was trying to make them all into mini-me's as servant leaders. That was clearly me trying to control behavior and was not possible as a sustainable solution.

"**Potential for Passivity:** Servant leaders tend to avoid taking a firm stance and making difficult decisions" (2023).

The first time I had to fire someone, I was a wreck. And I'm sure I kept employees who were not a good fit for longer than I should have because I was avoiding the hard decisions. Where it manifested with my larger guard force was in my desire to work with them on absenteeism and call-offs.

CALL-OFFS

Shift work is hard. There's little flexibility and no PTO. Vacation time was one week earned after a year. If my employees couldn't or didn't want to work, they would "call off." This was hands down the hardest part of the business to manage.

Looking at the big picture, there were times of the year when we could predict a spike in call-offs. As an example, who wanted to work on Father's Day or Mother's Day? Or graduation weekend? These were family-heavy events and didn't pay time and a half. Around the time of these major events, we got ready for the calls. But then there were everyday situations when employees were sick. Or their kids were sick.

Or the babysitter flaked. Or the car wouldn't start. My heart went out to them.

We allowed for call-offs. But I was caught in the push-pull of how to allow my employees to have time off for various personal issues yet still be able to staff my posts. Everyone on my management team knew the worst thing that could happen is that a post goes unmanned or "open." It was constantly a dance between the two to satisfy both employees and customers. And after a while, the policy was being taken advantage of, and we needed some more structure. So, we implemented a point system to hold the accountability. But I probably allowed way too much absenteeism, which I know drove up overtime costs and caused many scheduling issues.

It wasn't the best decision for my bottom line, but it was the best decision that aligned with my value system. Servant leader in action, for better or worse.

MAKING A DIFFERENCE
As the Institute for Management Development concludes its wrap up of this leadership style, "At its highest form, Servant Leadership prioritizes the needs of the employees and customers, which can increase employee motivation and job satisfaction, resulting in lower turnover rates and higher commitment and loyalty to the organization" (2023).

I would hope the series of small choices to show care and concern made a difference in my employees' lives and played out in better customer service to my clients. There was a reason I picked the logo with two shields representing both my customers and employees. The mission to protect my clients was completely on the efforts of my employees. And my role was to protect and value my employees to the very best of my ability. The fact that I could never pay them what they were worth just motivated me all the more to do what I could to respect and support the men and women who chose to work at Clarion. If that was my legacy, then for all the hard days and painful situations I faced, it was worth every last one of them.

Now we had the infrastructure in place to hire employees for our contracts. But I was soon headed up a side trail very early in our business cycle that would risk setting our company back. And that was being way too aggressive in our growth strategy, pushing for the latest and greatest technology to make us better and different from the competition. It was too much too soon. If I were climbing that mountain looking for the quickest trail up, I might have seen the sign if I looked harder. "Danger, trail closed. Take another route." But I wasn't paying attention to the warning signs. It seemed faster than the other trails up. I forged right ahead with tunnel vision.

Bleeding Edge Syndrome

"What is going on with this stupid car?" I asked myself. I gripped the steering wheel tighter and squared myself off in the seat, sitting stiffly upright so I could focus. It was 2:00 a.m., and I was driving back from handling a problem on an overnight shift. "It's going to die before I make it home!" I kept telling myself to calm down and think as the miles left on the battery charge kept ticking down in rapid-fire progression.

Fifteen miles to home. Twenty miles on the screen indicating miles remaining on the battery charge. The adrenaline shot through my system, and I coached myself up. *Cut the power points that are draining the battery. Turn off the radio, then the heat.* Five minutes later... ten miles to home, ten miles on the screen. *Okay, no choice. Cut the lights.* My eyes darted around the freeway frantically as I used the highway lights to assess the road for truckers that might not notice me. The car was tiny.

One mile to go. Zero miles on the screen. I willed the car to cooperate, *Please let me make it off the highway.* I coasted down the exit ramp, thankfully through a green light, then glided another fifty yards to a side road. That was all it had in it. A half mile from home, I shut it down. At least I wasn't on the highway dealing with a dead car. Or worse.

I was driving the first generation Nissan Leaf. The first battery-powered, reasonably priced car. According to A-1 Performance Auto, "The First Gen Nissan Leaf has difficulty in colder temperatures. When it gets cold outside you can expect a loss of 57 percent of your normal mileage" (2020). That was from a 2020 article. Who knew that in 2011? Not me until I experienced it the hard way.

According to Nefttagaz.Ru, "Cutting-edge technology refers to technological devices, techniques, or achievements that employ the most current and high-level developments, most advanced version of a product or service; in other words, technology at the frontiers of knowledge. The phrase cutting edge has a positive connotation and can be contrasted with the phrase bleeding edge, which has a negative connotation. Bleeding edge implies that a product or service is so new that its adoption could be harmful" (2021).

And we had a bad case of bleeding edge syndrome. We were trying so hard so fast to be fresh, innovative, and different that we crashed and burned a few times during those first few years. Circling the mountain, if you will. Chasing rabbit trails that stalled out as a dead end that depleted time, energy, and money.

CUTTING-EDGE STRATEGY

We had to be different. We knew that much. We could compete on price as we entered the market, but that wasn't a long-term strategy. How to stand out from the competition?

According to a blog post from the JDR Group, these are six ways to differentiate from competitors:

1. Distinctive sales offering
   a. Bring unique skills and background that add value to your particular service
2. Unique execution on the sales process
   a. Sales process
   b. Customer treatment
   c. Service delivery
3. Answer key customer problems
4. Be specific
   a. Focus on niche areas of competency
5. Make culture a priority
6. Step up your game in marketing
   a. Be bold, innovative, and radical (2019)

I had fresh eyes on the business and saw the opportunities immediately, which I would say contributed to developing a unique selling point. The guard business was somewhat stale in approaches and processes in general. Being an outsider was beneficial because I wasn't coming at the strategy from how "things were always done." I was looking at best practices from completely outside the industry. If I condensed those next categories into my cheat sheet of what made us so different and how that enabled us to grow as fast as we did, I would define my differentiators as follows:

Our unique execution — Two-hour go time.
Answer key customer problems — Death to paper.
Make culture a priority — Clarion cares.
Be specific — Guards and guards. The end.
Step up your game in marketing — Free and paid PR both work.

DEATH TO PAPER

"What do those daily activity sheets say?" I asked my supervisor as a stack of handwritten forms cluttered up the desk.

"It's all the daily activity reports from the last month the officers filled out while on the post," she responded. I glanced at a few. Handwritten documentation of times and rounds. I thought, *What's to prevent someone from writing out their rounds about thirty minutes before the end of the shift?* I went on to the next stack.

"What are those?" I said, frowning.

"Oh, that's the fifty-page report from the Deggy Guard Tour Wand that prints out the rounds each time you push the button."

I crossed my arms as I exclaimed, "That's just from one day?" My jaw was tensing up. I went on to the next giant stack. "What are those papers?"

He responded, "Oh, those are the incident reports from anything unusual that happened."

I scanned the one on the top of the stack that said the police had come on to the site the last night to respond to a burglar alarm coming from one of the buildings. Narrowing my eyes, I said, "Did we send this to the client and let them know?"

The supervisor hesitantly responded, "I'm not sure." I had heard enough.

In our research early on, we found a technology that automated that entire paper process. We could use the technology to create an automated site for each client. The really cool part was that we could code in "incident types" such as "trespasser," "vehicle break-in," "property damage," "emergency vehicles on site," "water leak," and so on. If a water leak was found, the guard could select that incident type, take a few pictures, type some commentary on their phone, and hit submit. It would then be sent immediately to the client, who would get the incident in real time, review the pictures and commentary, and be alerted to anything and everything happening on their site. Brilliant!

It would also be sent to supervisors and management in real time so we would be equipped with the knowledge as well if we needed to contact the client to discuss and give further detail. We could also code rounds with a date/time stamp. In real time, when guards were patrolling, they would take various pictures throughout their shift to document the work. It would be evident whether they were working or not. A paper report couldn't be manipulated anymore.

Licensing the technology was a game changer. We had secured a real, tangible way to deliver improved security performance to customers. The paper era was over for us. Eventually, the competition caught up, but not before we had already gained a significant advantage.

TWO-HOUR GO TIME
"We had an incident at the property and were wondering if you could send over a guard right now."

"The alarm system is down, and we need a fire watch for the holiday weekend."

"Our new warehouse is up and running, but the cameras haven't been installed. Can you provide 24/7 coverage for a month, starting tonight?"

"We need to replace the guard service working on the film production immediately and need ten guards at all filming locations tonight."

"Can you help us?" That's all I would hear when presented with such requests. Security doesn't wait. The calls come in when the needs arise. It's not convenient or easy. As I walked down the hall to the scheduler and operations manager to tell them what I had just committed the company to, they could already tell by the look on my face. It wasn't a case of "if"; it was a case of "when." And the only question was, "How long do we have to get someone there?" Would we have liked the ability to have weeks to start a job? Of course. But we were scrappy and responsive. Sometimes it taxed our resources to the max, but it caused us to win multiple contracts and retain clients who knew they could count on us to deliver.

CLARION CARES

From the Oxford Languages' definition of care:

1. The provision of what is necessary for the health, welfare, maintenance, and protection of someone or something.
2. Serious attention or consideration applied to doing something correctly or to avoid damage or risk (2023).

Security is a serious business. And we took it seriously. That attitude permeated our organization. We couldn't guarantee the results, but we could passionately commit to the approach and convey to our clients the importance we placed on protecting their property and people. It required that attitude from every level of the organization. Sometimes it was too much, and employees burned up and burned out. Or, other times, individuals failed to commit. But we never stopped defining our company by the standard of excellence of care.

GUARDS AND GUARDS. THE END.

There were so many fun diversions we toyed with over the years. Drones, cameras, and central station CCTV remote monitoring. Though, every time, I eventually snapped back to reality and regained my focus. We provide security guards. But I understand manned security guards are expensive, and there are times when clients don't believe they are getting an adequate return on that investment. Some clients want to go the route of camera technology. And it was appealing to dabble in that product offshoot. But cameras don't deter crime. They just show you the crime. Security guards deter criminals. Maybe not all the time, but I contend that if the criminal sees an armed guard standing on a property, they would perhaps be more likely to move along. I constantly looked for ways we could improve our service to add to that value. We had our hands full refining our security guard service. It wasn't easy, but that's where we started, and that's where I would stay. I was laser-focused on our niche.

"KIM HEATHCOTT: FACES OF MEMPHIS"

That heading was the title of a magazine spread in StyleBlueprint by Jennifer Chandler (2017). We were different. We drove orange Prius vehicles around town instead of the typical trucks that other security guard companies drove. A woman ran the business. Giving back to the community was paramount. We approached the industry in so many unique ways, which we made sure were well documented in media sources. In order to build a brand, there has to be a public awareness. We chose not to invest significantly in advertising dollars. But PR was paramount. Often we were nominated for some sort of small business award, and although not always the winner, many times we were a finalist, which allowed us to "sell ourselves" in the media page we were given to answer scripted questions. Once I got the maximum word count from the media source, I used every single word allotted for my company. When the publication was released, my answers were almost always twice as long as the other finalists. Why not? It was more publicity to let the entire city know how we were different and innovative.

CUTTING EDGE TO BLEEDING EDGE

We had built the model. It made sense, and we were winning clients. But then we got ahead of ourselves. If it was good, could we make it even better?

PRIUS VERSUS LEAF

Sustainability. Innovation. Clean energy. Hybrid fuel-efficient vehicles that were easy to drive and maximized gas mileage. We were doing great with our Prius vehicles. Then Tesla came out with its 100 percent battery-powered Roadster in 2008. Way out of our price range. Then the 100 percent battery-powered Nissan Leaf was introduced in 2010. "Just think how innovative we will be to have these in our fleet!" we thought. And just imagine, "No more gas expenses!" We didn't really think it through. A complete failure. Where were we going to charge it? We had to run the charging cord through a window at the office. Didn't really consider the logistics. Okay, this was trending badly. And then I wasn't the only one who ran the car down to nothing. My supervisor would be stuck across town with zeroes flashing. Time to call AAA to come tow it back to the office. The only saving grace was that we bought only one. And it performed so poorly that it was gone from the fleet in less than three months.

THE CLARIONWATCH 360 DEBACLE

We gathered at the marketing firm for our third meeting to figure out the name. "What do you want it to convey in the marketplace?" the PR team asked all so seriously. A name for a technology we hadn't even finalized yet. "Let's whiteboard some names to see if we can get a consensus on something fresh and different." All this just to come up with the *name* of our new technology. And thus ClarionWatch 360 was created.

We had decided to become our own technology company and create an app to replace the licensed technology and super improve it with all these new bells and whistles. I realize there are many companies that develop apps in their business models to become more efficient, which are highly successful. But we were one year into the business. It was a major strategy shift and capital drain. Now I had contracted with a third party to develop the app for a significant capital investment. And it was dragging on. I had gotten my operations manager involved, and he was interfacing with the India team, so we were both distracted.

Looking back, did we think we were going to license the technology to other security companies and transition away from guards? If we just used it in our business, I was never going to recoup the development costs with customers who weren't willing to pay any more for security services than the current market. It was just simply a terrible decision. The only saving grace is that I let the first version die after about eighteen months and didn't stubbornly try and keep going with it just to sink more capital into development.

It's not a bad idea to take business risks to push the envelope. We were just too fast and aggressive. Had we waited a few more years, perhaps it would have been more successful. Or perhaps we would have found a newer technology and saved ourselves a lot of time and energy that could have instead been devoted to the fundamentals of our business. And ultimately, that's what we did.

Thankfully, we got back to the basics so we could keep moving upward. But those were expensive lessons, not only due to the money wasted but also the time wasted that could have instead gone to trying to win more customers with a cutting-edge strategy that worked. Now we were about to pay the price. The cash was running out, which had the potential to stop us right in our tracks.

PART 2

BRAVING THE ELEMENTS

Financial Crisis

I heard the mail slide through the front door slot. It was late afternoon, and I had worked myself up into a frenzy. I had already checked my numbers a hundred times over. My biggest expense item—payroll— had been posted to my bank account that morning and was clearing at midnight, which would overdraw my business checking account by a significant sum. The funds available from the credit line at the bank weren't sufficient. Two plus two wasn't equaling six, which was what I needed to cover the cash. Where was my other "two" going to come from?

Kim, you are a former banker, and you've pushed it this tight? I sat there in a cold sweat mulling over my predicament. *You're supposed to know how to handle your operations profitably,* I berated myself. Or was it because I knew what I was doing, that I was gambling and playing it that close to the fire? I needed a cash bailout of some form, and the clock was ticking. I was desperately praying the money I needed that day would drop onto the floor of the front foyer. Gold in the form of customer payments. I had until 5:00 p.m. to make the deposit. I rushed up to the front door as soon as I heard the clink of the mail slot drop the bounty. Only... there weren't any checks in the stack.

The hole was *big*. Where would I find the cash to bridge us through this time around?

CASH IS KING

It is important to have a financial accounting system in place that shows you what profit you are making (or losing) in a company. But although that's one indicator of the financial health of your business, it's not the most important one. What you care about is that the cash doesn't run out.

And we were growing so fast that we were running out of cash. How could that happen? In the classic article "How Fast Can Your Company Afford to Grow?" by Neil C. Churchill and John Mullins, published in the *Harvard Business Review*, they lay it out as such: "Few people understand that a profitable company that tries to grow too fast can run out of cash—even if its products are great successes. A key challenge for managers of any growing concern, then, is to strike the proper balance between consuming cash and generating it. Fail to strike that balance, and even a thriving company can soon find itself out of business—a victim of its own success" (2001).

So how can the cash run out? Unfortunately, there are many ways. And if you experience more than one of the following, it makes it tremendously hard to keep the venture afloat.

1. Cash burn. Simply put, if you spend money in the business before you have enough revenue to cover the expenses, you may tap out or "burn" through all you have in the bank.

Often a startup company experiences this situation because the business infrastructure needs to be built before there is sufficient revenues to support the operation. According to CFI, "Burn Rate refers to the rate at which a company depletes its cash pool in a loss-generating scenario. It is a common metric of performance and valuation for companies, including start-ups. A start-up is often unable to generate a positive net income in its early stages as it is focused on growing its customer base and improving its product. As such, seed stage investors or venture capitalists often provide funding based on a company's burn rate" (CFI Team 2023).

Small businesses that are starting up may not have access to this type of funding. Especially in a service business when there's not a product to develop that needs significant outside capital. And typically, banks don't want to lend money to companies that have no track record. So where do you find enough cash to get you through until you have enough customers to cover operating expenses? It's called bootstrapping your business and leveraging your personal assets and possibly friends and family. That's the route I chose.

2. Working capital cycle cash crunch. If you grow and add customers (and have to add inventory if you're selling a product) but first have to make payroll and pay the rent and can't bridge the expenses until customers pay you, you may run out of cash. If you make the sales and don't invoice timely, or if something happens and your customer doesn't pay you,

you may run out of cash. If you have inventory on hand that customers don't want, then it won't sell, and if you don't receive the cash you invested in it, you may run out of cash.

As illustrated in a blog post from *Just Entrepreneurs*, written by Annabel Ah-Lim, there are three main steps in the cycle:

1. "Pay for assets (for example inventory to sell or equipment for a job).
2. "Sell inventory (or complete the job for a customer).
3. "Receive payment on what you've sold" (Ah-Lim 2023).

The working capital cycle is calculated as follows: "How long it takes to sell the inventory (inventory days) plus how long it takes to receive payment (Receivable days) minus how long you have to pay your supplier (Payable days)" (Ah-Lim 2023).

The collection of receivables can be managed well or poorly, and that drives collectability. You can manage payables by "stretching their payment" past the due date, but sometimes that's at your own risk. That could backfire if you continually push that strategy and they stop doing business with your company.

I didn't have inventory in my business, but some jobs required significant investments in equipment to get started. Golf carts, cars, guns, and uniforms. All up-front expenses. And my biggest payable was payroll. And that payout was clockwork every two weeks. Then there were my customers. It seemed like the bigger and more significant the customer was, the longer they took to pay. Fortune 500 companies were demanding and getting ninety-day terms. Getting a major new contract from a large corporation was a double-edged sword. I could pay out millions of dollars in up to nine payroll cycles before getting paid anything from them. That's an example of how aggressive growth can cause a company to run out of cash if not managed sufficiently. And we were pursuing these contracts just as fast as we could get them.

3. Consuming cash syndrome. If you use cash for property, equipment, or investments or to pay yourself and do not leave enough in the business, then you tap out.

You may need to purchase property or equipment necessary for your business. Or make investments in technology. Or purchase a building to operate in. All significant cash outlays may or may not be financed. If they are unfinanced, then that's a use of cash. How about if you own the business but don't take a salary? You make a distribution of cash for personal use. These are decisions that could significantly impact your cash flow. Especially if you are too aggressive because you see profits rising (on paper) and take out or use cash so that it drains your liquidity.

DEBT CAN BE OKAY
Debt is a source of cash.

"Kim, I never had a dime of debt, and I grew the business to $50 million." A business mentor, he wasn't so much bragging as stating his business philosophy. Then there was another business associate who told me her story. "Kim, we made money from day one. We never needed any debt." Well, that one stung. Both stories are amazingly admirable. Not to be defensive, but debt financing, if used in the right way, can leverage growth tremendously. It's all a balancing act. With my many years in commercial banking, I wasn't fearful of accumulating debt because I saw how business loans could be of value to the company in the right measure. Maybe my journey would have been different if I were debt averse, but I wasn't.

If companies have a commitment to growth, then a working capital line of credit can be a lifeline to the business. It can bridge that gap between the payment and the collection of income. With my first customers, I obtained a small working capital line of credit backed by the SBA (Small Business Association). Banks who wouldn't normally lend to companies in the startup phase may extend one of these products because the federal government guarantees the majority of the debt repayment (SBA: Small business Administration 2023).

Over the next ten years, I went back to the bank and increased the line every time we got a bigger contract. It enabled us to keep the rapid growth level going.

DEBT OR EQUITY? THAT IS THE QUESTION

When you go for a long time with a cash burn, it impacts the balance sheet of the company. And especially if you finance the cash burn with debt.

As Jeremy Salvucci explains, "A leverage ratio is a metric that expresses the degree to which a company's operations are funded by debt (borrowed capital). The most popular leverage ratio—the debt-to-equity ratio—compares a company's debt to its owners' equity. Companies whose operations are funded primarily through debt (in other words, companies with high debt-to-equity ratios) are described as being very 'leveraged'" (2023).

And yes, we were leveraged much higher than the typical gold standard in the lending business of 1:1. The 1:1 ratio means that you are equally financed by debt and equity. Oops, that was not us.

Salvucci goes on to say, "Leverage isn't necessarily a bad thing. It is normal for companies—especially newer companies and those in growth phases—to borrow capital in order to develop and expand. So long as payments are made on time, expansion can continue, and additional borrowing remains an option. That being said, the more debt a company carries relative to its equity and/or assets, the riskier of an investment it can be for shareholders. In the event a company's revenue isn't high enough to keep up with its debt, it may become insolvent and could even go bankrupt" (2023).

And I would add it is risky in the eyes of bankers. High leverage indicates there may not be enough liquidity in the business should anything cause a downturn in revenue or profits. I knew I was being aggressive with my debt financing. It happened at one of our quarterly bank meetings. "Kim, we think you may need to bring in some investors to get the balance sheet more in line." Here was my problem, though. I knew my pipeline. We were quoting on jobs that were significant. Those potential new customers were going to push our revenues up substantially and would solve the imbalance. But I was willing to play out the scenario. As I started meeting with investors, I realized it was the absolute worse time to give up any equity in the business and an amazingly good time for them to invest. And they knew it. I had some offers on the table, and I just couldn't stomach working that hard for these past five years and handing over ownership for a relatively small investment.

There had to be another way to manage the balance sheet until we got back to a more bankable scenario. And I found one. I factored my invoices for a year. It wasn't pretty, and it wasn't cheap. And I didn't like them at all. But they were a necessary evil. A factoring company purchases your receivables and gives you immediate payment less a discount fee. They don't care about your balance sheet. They only care about the ability of your customer to pay you. And we had a gold-standard customer list. I stayed with them for a year, and sure enough, the pipeline came through. We went right back to the bank and kept on growing. It was a painful solution, but I didn't give up any ownership. Again, creative debt financing on my part, but it worked. It was the path I chose to get out from under the issue.

WHAT HAPPENED TO THE CASH?

So why did I run out of cash that day? It was easy to see in retrospect. I tipped the balance way too far into consuming cash early on in the business.

MISTAKES IN BOOTSTRAPPING

Even though we started the business on a shoestring budget, I miscalculated how quickly we could ramp up our revenues.

Remember how security is a serious business? Well, decision-makers on the corporate and municipal side wouldn't be effectively managing risk if they handed out multi-million security contracts to an inexperienced operator. And that's what we were those first few years—unproven. Sure, we had a handful of clients that took a chance on us. But we were building a résumé, and landing a significant contract takes years to win. Early on, I invested in management personnel that assumed we would grow quicker than we did. That accelerated the cash burn.

INVESTMENT IN SOFTWARE

The software app was a 100 percent use of cash. And a bad decision. And made in 2011 while we were upside down with higher expenses than revenues. Another accelerant to the cash burn.

CASH DISTRIBUTIONS

It becomes problematic when your family is 100 percent dependent on one source of income, which is a startup operation. When the business generates a profit, you need to pull some cash from the business, which impacts liquidity. It was difficult navigating the balance. Hard choices were being made. Another adder to the cash burn.

GROWING MY WAY TO PROFIT

We turned the corner. Our company had an impressive résumé, an excellent reputation, and a diversification of clientele and security experience. There was only one way to go up to get out of this stall we had been in. And that was to rush the mountain as fast as possible. Grow, grow, grow. I had the working capital line, and it was time to make up for the ground we lost those first few years. It was aggressive, and it sometimes tripped us up in cash on hand.

But things evened out. After reaching that midpoint of the mountain, cash started catching up with growth. Revenues covered expenses. Cash distributions weren't wiping out liquidity. We could breathe. It had been way too long.

TIP FOR SUCCESS
Numbers are my jam. And I had years of experience in analyzing financial statements before becoming an entrepreneur. I've created business accelerator programs for small business entrepreneurs, where I discuss all these topics in depth. And my biggest concern among small businesses is the trend to outsource monthly financial statement preparation to accounting firms. I understand most entrepreneurs don't come from a banking background, but I strongly believe that if you give up oversight of the financials day to day, you also lose sight of the cash flow. Know your numbers. Manage your cash.

FINAL WORD
Although dicey at times, numbers eventually weren't my problem anymore. I was much better at solving the numbers than handling the people. And things on the people and property side were about to get intense.

Property Perils

"Is this the owner of Clarion Security?" said the voice on the other end when I answered the phone at about 1:00 a.m. one morning. "This is Officer Smith with the Memphis Police Department. I'm with your guard who has gotten his security vehicle stolen." *Really?* I was quite awake now. "Do you, by chance, have a way to track the car through GPS? He thinks you might."

Well, as a matter of fact, I did have a GPS on the car. At that point, we probably had about ten cars either patrolling around the city or patrolling around a client property. This was a first-generation GPS system, not as slick as the software we would eventually use. It was time to put it to the test. But first, what had happened? I called my officer to find out.

"Ms. Kim, I pulled into a gas station to get a snack. I stop there just about every night. I left the car running, and when I checked out, the car was gone. But I have the key! It's in my pocket." *Wow!* His post is in a really rough part of town, hence why they would need a security patrol. He then explained and justified his decision. "I know a lot of people in the neighborhood," which somehow made him feel comfortable enough to leave the car idling. He had a false sense of security when there should have been less flippancy in his attitude and more caution. That's what I thought, but not what I said.

I made no comment. I just needed that GPS to work. I fired up my laptop, and the GPS was still plugged into the car, throwing off a stationary location less than a mile from the gas station. I gave the police the address and stood by. About thirty minutes later, they called me back. "Mrs. Heathcott, we found the car parked in the driveway of a residence, and it had been turned off. No one is here. They've apparently abandoned it. What would you like us to do?"

Since my guard had the key, the criminals weren't able to get the car to function anymore, so they abandoned it. Haha, I guess the joke was on them. One lame-duck security car, nonfunctional for any more joyrides. Chalk one up for the hybrid car and the remote key and my first-generation GPS tracker.

So then I asked the police, "Can you let my guard just take the vehicle? He has the key." He was with them in the police car, and they were agreeable, so he got in the Clarion car and, five minutes later, was back to his patrol.

Situation resolved. We didn't lose a car. It wasn't even worth pressing charges. It was easier to just remedy the situation at hand and move on. Crisis averted, and I could go back to sleep. I don't think I even said a word to my guard about it. I knew he felt bad about the situation. It was kind of a no harm, no foul. But it did reinforce one of the lessons I had learned in a myriad of ways.

Employees often don't value company property as the business owner does.

My people matter. My people needed company property to do their job effectively. Depending on the assignment, it could be a portion or all of the following: Uniforms, badges, cell phones, computers, golf carts, vehicles, and guns.

My property matters. It's expensive to purchase and expensive to maintain.

So, did property matter to my people? And between the two, what choices did I need to make to balance them fairly and effectively? Were my policies showing I was leaning too much on the side of either people or property?

PEOPLE VERSUS PROPERTY

I've never been one to put unrealistic expectations on keeping possessions in pristine condition. Accidents happen, and my philosophy is that if you value the inanimate object more than the human who damaged it, then you've got the equation wrong. However, we were having many accidents:

- A new phone at the post gets dropped, and the screen cracks.
- The supervisor's laptop is left on the top of the vehicle and smashes into the street when the car drives off.

- A golf cart charger is plugged into an outlet in a guard shack and then driven off without unplugging it, busting the guard house window out.
- A new patrol car is picked up at the dealership at 5:00 p.m. The next morning it already has a dent on the passenger side.

My philosophy was being tested because I was starting to not be able to distinguish between mere accidents and gross negligence. If it were just accidents and one-off incidences, it wouldn't have bothered me so much. But the truth was I was battle scarred from multiple years, with multiple cars, multiple drivers, and multiple incidents. Four squared to the max. Nothing surprised me anymore.

"Ms. Kim, it was foggy this morning on the road, and a deer came out of the woods, and I ran directly into it. The deer ran off, but I'm looking at the car, and I'm pretty sure the car is totaled."

"Ms. Kim, I don't know what happened." The patrol supervisor then explained, "The phone fell on the floorboard, and when I was reaching for it, I ran a stop sign and slammed into the retaining wall at the end of the street. I think the car may be totaled." Hmmm... So maybe it was an accident, but was it really negligence?

"Ms. Heathcott. Your guard parked the golf cart on top of a small hill without the parking brake engaged. It rolled slowly all the way down to land in the side of one of our employee's cars." Was this an accident or was it negligence?

"Hey, I looked at your car regarding that engine light, Mrs. Heathcott." The automotive serviceman went on, "It seems as if the car never had an oil change and is bone dry. Since the car has about 20,000 miles on it, I'm pretty sure the engine has burned up." That car had probably had the engine light on for months, with every driver staring at that light and never saying a word about it. Yep, definitely negligence.

I had a hundred more stories just like these. But it wasn't just the complete destruction of vehicles. It was a slow death of computers, phones, golf carts, and vehicles. They don't call them depreciating assets for no reason. My people were de-accelerating the heck out of their value at a dizzying pace.

POLICY

According to a blog post from PaperTrails, their recommendation would be, before actually distributing company property to employees, to make sure to have a clearly defined policy in your employee handbook. Sample generic wording might include the following:

"An employee is expected to exercise due care in his/her use of company property and to use such property only for authorized purposes. Willful misuse or negligence in the care and use of company property will be considered cause for suspension and/or dismissal. The employee may be held responsible for repairing or replacing any damage to equipment due to willful misuse and/or negligence" (2023).

We had an employee handbook. We had a clearly stated policy similar to the example. But looking back, I had two big issues driving behavior that I needed to address. And one conflicted with the other.

1. Property was mostly issued to a post and not to a person, which caused carelessness to turn into negligence.
2. Employees did not have sufficient resources to handle property issues.

POST PROPERTY

Most of our posts had multiple officers and multiple shifts. In a week's time, there could be ten to fifteen different people driving a golf cart or company car or using a company phone. We had to leverage those assets across the client site. It blurred the lines of employee accountability. Each person was supposed to inspect and record any issues with the equipment when handed down to them. But, over time, I found that if they noticed issues, they weren't being reported.

"Hey, why is the new golf cart cover stuffed in the back of the golf cart crumpled and dirty?" We had just bought a new one two days prior, which had been perfectly placed on the cart to keep bad weather out. "I'm not sure," was the response. "Do you know who took it off?" No one ever did. It was a mystery.

It seemed like many of these incidences were crossing over from accident to negligence bordering on willful negligence and damage. Or maybe I was starting to be weary from the sheer volume of them. And I started feeling personally offended at the carelessness of it all. I thought, *If behavior was going to change, there would have to be a cost.* If it was a clear-cut incident, I would have the officer pay a portion of the repairs out of his or her paychecks over a period of time.

And we revised the policy. But we were careful to do the legal research. Not only did the employee have to acknowledge the damage, but we had to determine a fair and reasonable repayment plan and amount. As stated by Davidson Morris, "Employers must also act reasonably regarding how much they take from their employee's wages. The amount deducted per pay period must be reasonable with respect to the employee's earnings. What is considered being 'reasonable' is determined on a case-by-case basis, and largely depends on the employee in question" (2023). And we knew that any offset to their income could not take them below minimum wage.

Which led me to my next issue.

EMPLOYEE RESOURCES
The majority of my employees didn't have adequate resources to absorb 100 percent of repair costs. If we found they totaled a car out of negligence, there was no way they could ever really pay me back, even for the insurance deductible. It was mostly the principle of the matter for asking them to pay a portion for what they damaged. Because, in execution and to be financially reasonable, it needed to be on a payment plan and a very low deduction number. And the employee could leave the company without ever paying it back, and there was not any recourse for that.

What I was finding out was that the policies weren't really helping me drive behavior change. It was then I just decided to chalk it up to the cost of doing business. I just had to be smarter and wiser. *If a GPS device was going to be pulled out of a car to eliminate tracking, then I'll hardwire it into the car, and there will be no box, but my software will work just fine.* I think it was just getting ahead of the game. I wouldn't take it personally because the only attitude I could change was mine. I couldn't care so much that my employees cared less. I couldn't control behavior, but I could manage it in some ways. That was the lesson for me.

Looking back, I didn't do a good job of matching consequences with behavior. For the guard who drove that car with the engine light on, day in and day out, slowly burning the car engine up, was it really their fault? Or was it the fault of the operations manager tasked with checking the vehicle fleet for not observing it? Or was it my fault for not following up with the managers for not checking the vehicles properly?

It's easy to assign blame to someone else. It's hardest to look in the mirror and accept the responsibility started with me and my inconsistent management of firm policies and procedures. I decided I wasn't going to value the inanimate objects used in our business more than my people. But, at the same time, I didn't hold my people accountable for property management with fair and firm discipline. So, far too much property had been destroyed, and too little progressive discipline had been enforced in order for the entire employee base to understand that company assets were valuable and important to maintain.

As wisely stated in an article from PaperTrails, "Instead of deducting employee wages for damages, addressing the carelessness as a performance concern is a more appropriate response. Disciplinary action, such as a verbal warning or work suspension, may be necessary. If an employee is repeatedly damaging company property, termination may be required. As with any employee and employer interaction, it is extremely important to be consistent with company policy and document everything!" (2023).

Let's go back to the stolen Clarion car I discussed earlier. I didn't say anything to the guard—which, at that moment, was okay to do. But it should have been followed up on, documented, and discussed with him at the appropriate time soon thereafter. No harm, no foul is not a best practice. That would be a lesson that could be applied to any business with even one employee. You can't control behavior. You can set standards and write policies to support them to hold people accountable. And a good leader executes on that plan fairly and consistently.

It was one thing to deal with property issues. It was a whole different level having to manage issues affecting people and property beyond your control. Winter was coming, and the weather was very much out of my control.

Ice Wars

"If your post is not closed for the weather, you are expected to be on your shift. Leave early and drive slow."

If that sounded mean to some of my employees, it probably was supposed to come across that way. I was using my stern "I'm not kidding" voice. The voice that parents use when they want to scare their kids straight into behaving properly for a big event. Every one clocking out the day before the storm would hear the message and be warned. "Don't even try and start backing out of your schedule" is what my words were implying in my short, snappy, no-nonsense tone. I had to preempt the crisis about to erupt and set high expectations for my employees because we didn't have the flexibility or latitude to shut down posts. The city might be shutting down tomorrow, but Clarion Security would be business as usual. And to be business as usual, my people had to show.

Once everyone was warned, it was time to gather troops and arm the supervisors and managers with our weapons of ice destruction: kitty litter, ice scrapers, and four-wheel drive vehicles. They were meager weapons against the potential force of mother nature. But that was all we had. There was nothing to do now but wait out the storm front. We were on defense. I went to sleep, awaiting the storm's icy toll and its impact on the next morning's first shift at 6:00 a.m., mentally steeling myself for what lay ahead. It was not going to be pretty. It never was.

Most people, when they see a forecast of snow or ice, delight in the anticipation of the beautiful snowflakes and opportunities to stay at home. Kids home from school playing and sledding. The peaceful calm and stillness after a layer of snow and ice blankets the trees and yards.

Me? I watched the forecast with a mixture of dread and anxiety. I had dealt with tornados, heat, and heavy rainstorms, but snow and ice were my worst nightmare. Especially because in Memphis, these cold fronts would come in with temperatures dropping throughout the hours. And once the temperature hit 32 degrees, the weather would shift from rain to icy sleet. Covering the trees, bringing down power lines, and covering streets with ice that made it impossible to navigate. Black ice.

According to the National Weather Service, "Black ice is a deadly driving hazard defined as patchy ice on roadways or other transportation surfaces that cannot easily be seen. It is often clear (not white) with the black road surface visible underneath. It is most prevalent during the early morning hours, especially after snow melt on the roadways has a chance to refreeze over night when the temperature drops below freezing. Black ice can also form when roadways are slick from rain and temperatures drop below freezing overnight" (n.d.). And that was what typically happened with one of these ice storms.

I was blessed these conditions usually only came around for a few weeks each year. But, when they did, the result was impactful on our business operation. "I can't get my car door open to come to work. It's completely frozen shut." or "I live north of town, and there is a foot of snow up here. I can't get out of my driveway." And there were the calls that were always going to come in, despite my nastygram of a speech the day before. "I am not driving in this weather." From my viewpoint, I had a few choices. I could make a guard stay on post if their relief didn't show up. I hated that idea. Or I could have the post go open. That was even worse. So, I picked the third option and mobilized the troops. All my ops team, my family members, and I were going to pick up the employees who couldn't get to the post. We were going to war with ice.

Looking back, I didn't have to handle the storm this way. I didn't have to treat this like a war. Calamities happen. Clients understand. You communicate and do the best you can, and if there are failings, you accept responsibility and move on. That's probably what a more established, larger company would have done to handle this situation. But I had a chip on my shoulder. I wanted to prove we were better than our peers; to prove we would leave it all on the field for our clients; to prove I wouldn't give up and use excuses for a poor showing. When the going got tough, the tough got going. That's how I had lived my life, and it colored all my decisions. We were in crisis mode, and nothing was going to stop me from bullying our way through the bad weather.

And now it was here. The storm had arrived overnight, and the weather conditions were bad. Mostly ice with a bit of snow on top, which created extremely hazardous driving conditions. Even an inch of ice wreaked havoc, and this was a few inches. The call-outs started coming in around 5:00 a.m. Who was going to win? Was it going to be mother nature? *Not this time*, I vowed. I would not let this ice storm take us down without a fight. I took a deep breath and got in my car to head to the office to meet my assembly of snow drivers and galvanize the troops. We would take home employees, pick up employees, and stand posts. I delivered the message, and my team understood the mission. Whatever we could do to get everyone rolling on the first shift. Then perhaps we could have a respite until it would all start again that afternoon at shift change.

On that day, I felt like Mel Gibson as William Wallace, galvanizing the troops and leading his men into battle. It wasn't tyranny versus freedom. But it was a fight to prove we weren't going to give up in the face of formidable odds. I wasn't going to run a company where we ran from our problems and made excuses. We were going to go headlong into the fray to see if we could come out victors on the other side.

The battle plan was drawn up. I assigned the places everyone needed to go to pick up officers, then we all headed out. Only a few hours in, it was chaos on all sides. I got a call from my son, who I had recruited to fight the ice with us. He had driven out to pick someone up and lost control of his Tahoe on the ice and skidded into another car. We had no time to deal with his accident.

He exchanged insurance information and kept moving. Everyone understood the priority was getting officers to their posts.

Plus, I couldn't do anything to help my son because I was in the midst of the fray with my own issues. I was on my way to get an officer who needed to go home and had no ride. She had been sitting there for two hours waiting on someone to come get her. I picked her up and headed to South Memphis to take her to her apartment. We skidded on top of the ice around the cloverleaf highway by the Memphis Airport but were able to keep going without hitting the guardrail. I got to her apartment entrance and saw that her apartment was in the back of the parking lot, down a steep hill. I watched a car try and go up the hill and slide multiple times before getting some traction on the west side and was finally able to get up and out. We both watched, and neither of us said a word. It was like a roller coaster, where you are headed up slowly, and at the top of the hill, there are a few seconds where you stop and catch your breath at the overhang because it's all about to drop out from underneath you. I knew what she was thinking—I was thinking the same.

If I went down that hill to her door, could I get back up? I couldn't get stuck in her apartment complex. I was needed across town to handle another crisis. But then, how could I not go down the hill and make her walk 100 yards across the ice? I was at the overhang, suspended in reality. *What to do?* Then, my momentum pulled us along, and off we went. I skidded down the hill and kept tapping my brakes, praying I wouldn't slide and come to a stop careening into one of the parked cars. We skidded about twenty feet without hitting any of the cars and came to a stop still a good sixty yards from her door. The officer sensed I was in a quiet panic.

As the car came to a stop, she said, "Ms. Kim, I'll just walk home the rest of the way." And I let her do so because all I was focused on was how I was going to get back up that hill. I watched her slowly make it home safely. She gave me a thumbs up, then I turned the car and took the path I saw the other car take that had successfully escaped. It took me about three times, but I got my car up the hill. Then I was back out and running street duty.

By the end of the day, we were able to patch the posts together with only a few tough spots. Clarion won the day. But icy weather would come back around every few years, bringing different versions of pain along with it.

I had snow and ice PTSD—for years. It was hard enough to get 100 percent of posts covered week after week. These weather situations often seemed insurmountable. But somehow, we always made it through. I could have never done that by myself. It's like being in battle. You've got to have your team with you and behind you. And mine were always there for me. I would not ask them to do for me something I wouldn't do myself by leading the charge. Going up and down that hill that one icy day was just a metaphor for the journey this company had caused me to be on from the beginning, staring down the barrel of a difficult situation and pushing my way back out of it.

Winter storms caused a crisis for us in service delivery. Small businesses face versions of these storms all the time that may have nothing to do with the weather. It could be a cybersecurity attack crippling the operation. An employee strike. A product recall. A technology failure. A restaurant kitchen fire. Anything that unexpectedly causes issues that may seem insurmountable at the time. It's these times that test the leader's perseverance and commitment to managing through difficulties without giving up and learning how to pull together the team to tackle them head on.

John Maxwell writes about teamwork using the "Law of Mount Everest," which states that as the challenge escalates, the need for teamwork elevates. And as he points out,

- *"If we try to tackle challenges alone, we'll only spiral into failure.*
- *Our goals are still achievable, but we may need to adjust the teams we're relying on to help us reach them"* (2020).

We managed through these ice storms, but my team and I were fraying at the edges. I was pushing my team based on unrealistic expectations of performance. These weather events were exposing that while I tried to have control over insurmountable situations, there are times when it's flat-out impossible. I could cheerlead, motivate, and troubleshoot, but my best efforts wouldn't be enough to manage through without accidents and issues.

And my team was suffering from internal damage from the intense pressure I was applying to maintain our level of customer service despite business disruptions. The battles I would soon face would not be against mother nature but instead the dysfunctions of miscommunication, disappointment, and pride.

Would I make it any further with my team in danger of falling apart from the intense pressure I was applying on all sides?

Holiday Meals

"Mom, the gate is locked, and I can't get in."

The museum was locked up tight. The alarms were set. A beautiful building surrounded by acres of landscaped grounds. Not a soul in sight except for the security guard on the vast property. There was a button you could push on the gate, but no one answered. I knew the guard was there, tucked away inside at the main desk watching the surveillance camera.

"Hold on," I said. "Let me call her." I called the main number, no answer. Then I checked the schedule to see who was there. When I got the security guard's name, I called her cell phone. "My daughter is at the gate with a lunch for you."

It took a few minutes more for the guard to exit the museum and walk down the winding path to the gate. The Styrofoam container with lunch was handed off, and then my daughter headed to the next stop down the street, following the Christmas morning delivery route I had given her.

It was not going to be a leisurely morning lounging at home, enjoying the sights and sounds of Christmas morning. My kids were needed for the all-hands call in the field. This year, it was go time for our family of four. My kids were seventeen and nineteen, and they were needed as critical drivers for the mission at hand. To-go boxes were set up, covering every space in the kitchen. Ham and potato salad was pulled out of the refrigerator. Rolls and brownies on the counter. Red and green markers at the ready for my daughter to write "Merry Christmas, the Heathcotts" on the inside of the plastic containers. A list with all our posts divided into "North," "South," "East," and "West" on the map and how many lunches were needed for officers who were working on Christmas Day. The assembly would be prepped and ready around 10:00 a.m. Kids awakened. Clarion supervisors started arriving for their lists. I would hand out the destinations, and off we drove. This was our new Clarion Christmas morning tradition.

Security is often a lonely business. Giant facilities empty out on Thanksgiving and Christmas. Often, the only person or people on-site are the security guards tasked with overseeing an empty campus or building. Spending their holiday at work for eight-plus hours a day while everyone else enjoys time with families and friends. Delivering a holiday meal to the officers on post during those two holidays was our family's way of expressing our gratitude and showing that we appreciated their sacrifice. It was part of the culture we instilled from the beginning. A small gesture we hoped would convey the appreciation we felt. I hadn't had to employ my children until the last few years because we had grown so big. We didn't know that Christmas morning would be the last meal delivery we undertook as a company.

EMPLOYEE PERKS

Thanksgiving and Christmas meal deliveries were actually the last remnant of a perk started at the outset of the business. Providing meals to every officer on every shift that they worked was the Clarion way in the very beginning. In those early days, we decided that if we provided a meal to employees, it would accomplish two things. First, it would show the security officers we cared about them; and second, it would provide an opportunity for the supervisor to check on the officer and ensure they were on post, dressed in uniform, and handling duties as expected. For most posts, once a guard is on a shift, they can take a short lunch break but can't leave the post.

According to *USA Today*, "When it comes to employee perks, few things are as simply satisfying as free food and drinks—which, it turns out, are also just good business. According to a new survey by grocery-delivery service Peapod, companies that provide free food have happier employees compared with those who don't get to chow down on their employer's dime. While the majority, 56 percent, of full-time employees are 'extremely' or 'very' happy with their current job, that number jumps to 67 percent among those who have access to free food, the survey of more than 1,000 full-time office workers found. Though just 16 percent of employees said they get free snacks and treats at work" (2015).

Free food (health and wellness) is just one example of a perk that a company can provide. There are a variety of employee perks that can be offered to employees. Take a look at Quantum Workplace for an expanded sample of offerings that span these five major categories:

- Health and wellness
- Family
- Community
- Office environment
- Employee development (2020)

The key for companies, when they formulate which perks to offer, is to ask, "For what purpose?" As explained by Jocelyn Stange, "Perks don't have a direct impact on engagement. However, when planned strategically, they can support your engagement initiatives by reinforcing your company values and culture and building an employer brand that attracts and retains talent" (2020).

For us, delivering meals was what we chose to offer that seemed to align directly with our mission and values. In those early days when we were a startup, we figured that by offering this perk, we would convey the culture of "Clarion cares." Our employees often couldn't leave their shift for lunch. And they were tight on money. It seemed a win-win. And none of our competitors were doing anything like this.

THE RISE AND FALL OF SANDWICHES

Ah, to be one of our early employees was a culinary treat! We knew that we were delivering only sandwiches, so we picked a lunch provider. I picked what I thought were the best options, and we tried to have a variety. We picked a combination of cold and hot sandwiches. When we started, we only had about four customers. Only one had a dedicated lunch guard on the weekends. But fast forward a year later, and we had an operations bottleneck. We had grown substantially, and the volume had increased—and so had the geographic boundaries. By this time, there were employees who had food restrictions, and we decided we needed to simplify. We would just offer turkey sandwiches.

According to Grammarist, "Too much of a good thing means an excessive amount that becomes overwhelming or harmful, rather than helpful or pleasurable. In small amounts, the thing in question would be good for you or entertaining; in large amounts, the thing is harmful or a burden" (2023). And thus, after four years, turkey sandwiches crossed that line. Our guards were sick of turkey sandwiches. I would go by a post and see an unopened sandwich from the prior day. Or there was one time when we delivered the sandwich at the same time the pizza delivery guy showed up. I understand. I would be sick of them too. But what could we do instead? And how could I renege on that perk? Once you provide a benefit, how do you renege on it without creating disappointment?

I decided I had to offer an alternative that was more palatable (no pun intended!) to my employees. And it wasn't going to be a meal. It would need to be something better. And I decided there's nothing better than money. That's what I decided to lead with. I sent out a survey asking if my employees would rather receive a bonus than a turkey sandwich. I knew it would pass. And with that, sandwiches were out. That is, except for Thanksgiving and Christmas.

THE RISE AND FALL OF HOLIDAY MEALS

I felt like those holidays needed a personal touch that would be meaningful to the guards working. The only food choice those two days was McDonald's. I know because a couple of times when we ran short, I sent the roving supervisors to McDonald's as a backup. But those guards who worked those holidays couldn't leave the post to even make a McDonald's run. Even though by 2016, we had over 300 employees, I wanted the culture to still feel like a compassionate, family-run business. We wanted a holiday meal that would be representative of what many families might serve for a holiday meal.

For Thanksgiving, it was ham, potato salad, rolls, and pumpkin pie. For Christmas Day, it was the same menu, only subbing out the pie for brownies. At first, we provided meals for all three shifts that day 24/7, but as our numbers grew, I cut it to just the lunch meal. In my mind, I justified it that if someone worked overnight on Christmas Eve, getting off at 6:00 a.m., they could still be with their families for Christmas morning.

For the first three or four years, the holiday routine was manageable and didn't impact our family celebrations. But, around 2015, I would have the routes and to-go boxes packaged up and realized it was too much for the supervisors to deliver on a timely basis. The last thing I wanted was for an employee to be handed a to-go box at 01:45 p.m. with an end shift at 02:00 p.m. What good was that? It was a wasted effort.

So, I started helping the supervisors and taking a route on Thanksgiving and Christmas mornings. I loved doing it. Christmas morning was often a brisk, sunny day. I always picked the Northwest quadrant headed downtown and backtracking by our post near Graceland. No cars on the highway.

There was a peaceful calm as I headed to my guards. They were always there, whether sitting in a car, a deserted building, or a guardhouse access with no one to let in or out. I loved being able to hand them a meal and thank them for their work. In the early days of the business, I knew all my employees and was able to talk to most of them. But at 450 employees there were so many I had never met. It was an opportunity to make that one-on-one connection again in a small way.

I was just thankful. It made my holidays more meaningful that they were shared with some of my employees and that we were extending our thankfulness to some of them in a personal way.

In the last two years that we assembled and delivered Thanksgiving and Christmas meals, my entire family was needed. It was all hands on deck. Thank goodness my children were tech-savvy. I had the addresses and quantities listed in the delivery order, and they found the posts and people eventually. I know it was impactful on them to be a part of the process. The last thing they really wanted to do was to get dressed on Christmas morning and spend two hours on the road, but they never complained. I believe their hearts were also touched with compassion and thankfulness to the guards who received the meals. And my employees were so kind to them in return.

As hard as it was to run the company in so many ways, holiday meals were the absolute high point of my experience. It was the best of all of us coming together for our employees in an impactful way: Protecting customers. Valuing employees.

Holiday meals existed until 2017. Painful situations were playing out, and when it came to the holidays, I realized the meal delivery tradition would have to end. As with the turkey sandwiches, I had to offer something better. I decided that instead of a meal, every employee that worked on Thanksgiving and Christmas would receive double pay for hours worked. I could then expand it back to everyone. It would cost more out of my pocket, which would be sacrificial from a monetary standpoint versus a time and energy standpoint. It felt like the right thing to do.

It's hard when you are scaling a business and transforming it into more of a corporate company than a family-run business. Meals were the last place where I was still on the field with everyone. But as I evaluated the best strategy, it seemed like the right time to break that last family tie and replace it with a perk that was more scalable but still fit with our core values. I realized at those watershed moments that I could embrace the change presented in the circumstance that still aligned with the goals and values of the overall company. It's *not* a defeat; it's a shift.

PART 3

FIGHTING THROUGH SETBACKS AND STRUGGLES

Parking Lot Wars

"Ma'am, is that your vehicle parked in the handicapped space?" the policeman asked me politely.

I jumped as I didn't see him walk up behind me. It was 4:30 p.m., and I was sitting in the lobby of my new office, signing some papers. I had dashed in for a five-minute stop, and the parking lot was full. That was, except for the one spot right in front of my door: the handicapped space. I am normally such a rule follower, but the wheels of rationalization were turning in my mind. *It will be less than five minutes,* I justified. *Plus, there's a handicapped space right at the end if, by some random chance, someone needed to park there.*

"Officer, yes, I'm so sorry. I'm leaving right now." As I followed him out, three thoughts were running through my mind, which caused my blood to boil. One was, *This is just so random. We are in the back of three buildings. Someone had to have called the police on me.* There was no way he was driving into office parks chasing down handicap parking violations. Who would have done that? Well, I had a theory. I was pretty sure it was the business owner whose parking spaces we had been fighting over for the last few weeks. *I can't believe my neighbor just called the cops on me because I parked in the handicapped space!* Then my face got flushed as I thought, *Wow, I've been here just for five minutes. He got here that fast as if it was an active shooter situation. Really, like I'm the hot criminal?* And the final thought was, *Of all the crimes taking place in that very moment around the city, my neighbor felt it was necessary to call me on the carpet to teach me a lesson and waste the time of a public servant put in the middle of a petty parking lot fight?*

In business, there are big problems and small problems— major unexpected crises and small issues that repeatedly pop up and get under your skin and cause you to make poor decisions because you have an emotional reaction. I dealt with really difficult situations in my ten years of running my company— deaths, accidents, injuries, etc. Real life and death decisions. And now there was this. Parking lot melodrama. Every time I pulled into my office park for years, I allowed the unresolved drama to darken my demeanor and put me in a bad mood. And it wasn't just about parking spaces. It was because I was having a power struggle over them with my neighbor.

2014

We were moving on up! We had outgrown our starter office many times over. I was finally ready to commit to signing a long-term lease to accommodate our growth. We were bursting at the seams, and it was way past due. And the new digs were conveniently located one building over from my current office. The landlord let us design the facility, pick out paint and carpet, and custom tailor it to our business model in exchange for a five-year lease. After four months of remodeling, it was finally ready.

My landlord stopped in while we were packing for the move. "Kim, here are your new keys. Let's walk through the new office and make sure everything is ready." He was friendly and energetic, seemingly as excited as I was. As an afterthought on the walk back, he said "Hey, just so you know, over the weekend we are going to repave and restrip the entire parking lot."

"Perfect!" I responded. It was all coming together. Except for the one detail he neglected to share with me, which slapped me in the face as soon as I pulled up to the building Monday morning.

Glaring at me were four shiny, skinny cylinders of steel cemented to the back of the freshly tarred surface of four parking spaces in front of the building. I drove closer so I could see what the little square signs said on each. It was so clear once I got close. "Reserved." Reserved exclusively for my neighbor's business. Not one of the other twenty-five tenants of the office park had any reserved spaces, including me. Just the ones right next to my new office.

I whipped out my phone as soon as I put the car in park to call the landlord. "Why would you reserve four spaces for my neighbor?" He stammered out his response. "Well, she knew you had a lot of employees and vehicle traffic, and it's very important she has enough space for her customers." I was now fuming as I worked this over in my head. *Okay, yeah, but the math didn't work.* I was not done lambasting my property manager over the decision.

I went on lecturing him in full-steam fury. "But she has no employees and only small groups stopping by throughout the day. I have seven full-time office employees, patrol supervisors in and out, extra vehicles, training sessions, orientations, and various and sundry of my hundreds of employees dropping by for whatever they needed. Not to mention my applicants!" I always tended to argue in numbers and logic. The math didn't add up, and if he knew it, he wasn't giving an inch. I was outraged and felt totally justified unloading on my landlord.

And therein lied the problem. I bet for the four months that we were finishing out the space, my new neighbor had a sense of dread we were about to invade her space. She drove past our old location every day for two years and knew that hubbub of activity was about to descend on her quiet space. She had group sessions at odd hours and wanted to ensure the people attending the sessions were able to park right in front of her door. Okay, I guess that made sense. But, at the time, I didn't care about her perspective. I only cared about my new problem at hand and feeling blindsided.

"For those three or so hours of a ten-hour business day, her people are parked conveniently close to her door. But the rest of the day, the spots are completely empty. You've tied up four spaces that could be used all day long by my company." I kept arguing by analyzing and pitching the numbers in my defense. It wasn't going to get me anywhere, though. He'd cut a deal with her and probably had done so months before. She'd been a long-time tenant. I get it. If I were in her shoes, I would probably do the same. I say that now. But I was spitting venom then.

Why do I mention such a petty issue? Or one better, why did I let such a petty issue get the best of me? As I look back, the whole situation was a big lesson for me in negotiation, interpersonal dynamics, and conflict. We weren't the most important tenant in the office park. In a lot of ways, our company was probably the most aggravating. Being a security company with that high level of activity, we probably were a big crime deterrent for our neighbors, but I doubt that's how they viewed us. More likely, they saw us as the problem child of the office park—busy and chaotic, infringing on their much smaller business footprint. From my landlord's perspective, he was trying to pacify my neighbor, all the while rejoicing he had filled a big vacancy in his office landscape. His retort to me was, "Kim, you both essentially have the same square footage in each of your respective businesses. There are other places to park. She has four spaces in front of the building, and so do you." Four plus four equals eight. And that was the end of that negotiation.

I had started with arguing. Then I spent the next six years avoiding. And never once did I consider collaborating. I guess I didn't want to stop being mad. I never even had a single conversation with my neighbor. I didn't want to get to know her as a person and maybe be forgiving. Ah, grudges are the worst. And they are so exhausting to keep up. But I managed to nurse that grudge until I was able to move the company to another office park with an abundance of empty parking spaces, and my neighborly trials and tribulations eventually became a distant memory.

CONFLICT RESOLUTION

There are six main conflict resolution styles that range in assertiveness and cooperation. The "conflict avoider" is at the lowest point of both of those categories, with the "collaborative," problem-solving style being at the highest.

As detailed with great insight in an article from the professional mediators at Martha's Vineyard Mediation Program (MVMP),

> *The avoid stance is a lose-lose approach. That's because the two people who have a conflict don't get to share their concerns, negotiate, and develop understanding, and because of this, both parties lose out. Although many people have a negative view of conflict, the process of working conflicts out can be a net positive. Working toward a win-win or at least a compromise is all about learning, growth, and improved outcomes for both parties. We only make improvements through the process of struggle. Our view is that all human advancement is the result of conflict that is resolved, sometimes through trials and tribulations, but ends up with something better at the end.*
>
> *The lose-lose part of avoid is when there are real deeply-felt conflicts that are just buried. Or more accurately, like the ostrich, the head is buried while the conflict sits there, unresolved, unaddressed, and growing over*

time. Avoiding handling conflicts does not make them go away. Many people who are most comfortable with avoiding conflict may have little confidence in their own abilities to articulate their thoughts. Or they may have learned that avoidance is the best and most honorable way to go. But when someone lives a life of trying to avoid conflicts, they do catch up. And the consequent process of trying to avoid dealing with issues creates a lifestyle of fear. Not a recipe for a fully realized life well-lived (MVMP 2020).

Ouch. And that's exactly what happened. We were mere steps from each other physically, but neither of us ever reached out to take that first step figuratively—until I moved away, never to cross paths again.

A RECIPE FOR DISASTER
Every day of those six years, my irritation simmered in a low boil every time I passed those four empty spaces on the way into my office. Upon reflection, it all seems so ridiculous now. If I could go back in time, I would have set up a meeting with the landlord and my neighbor and tried to come to some sort of compromise. Maybe something might have changed; maybe not. Discussing the issue and airing out the emotions almost always deflates the negative air. But I wanted to hold on to the anger I felt toward the bait-and-switch my landlord had pulled and the anger I felt when my neighbor called the police. Which was never confirmed, but my intuition told me that's what happened. It was all so unjust in my mind that I didn't want to be the bigger person. Isn't that the way it always is? We wait for the other person to come to us with

an apology because, in our minds, we've been wronged. They *should* feel bad and want to resolve it. That's what we tell ourselves to keep us justified as the victim. But that self-talk is only that: to make us feel better simmering around in a sauce of resentment cooked up and served over a plate of prideful sulkiness.

Life is full of little problems just like that. The only choice we have is to change our attitude and thoughts about it. Bottling up resentment toward a person is not a healthy way of handling conflict. And I was about to get into some problems with some of my employees who were headed into conflicts that could possibly have been avoided. Unfortunately, I wasn't equipped at the time with healthier interpersonal skills. That sauce was about to spill out and ruin quite a few relationships within my company. And then ruin more personally.

THE STALL
In terms of climbing the mountain, it's as if I spent days and days hiking and then realized at the end of a long trek that I had circled back and was standing exactly in the same place I started. I had expended a lot of energy but never moved closer to the destination. I was worn out and discouraged, and so was my team. We were all carrying baggage that was hindering us from moving forward, and I blamed the map, the signposts, and the external markers for the error instead of taking responsibility for the issues myself.

I was stuck circling the mountain again and again. It would take a few more situations to finally cause me to assess what

I was doing wrong and where I could unload some of those bad habits, learn, regroup, and start moving back up.

Unhinged

I set the clip up in advance. I knew exactly where to start. It was the penultimate scene from *Mad Max Beyond Thunderdome*. The one where the crowd swells around the chamber as Tina Turner's character enters the chaotic madness. The titular "Thunderdome" is a death chamber, and a battle is about to unfold for all to observe.

The clip was set up for the TV in the conference room. About ten people were assembled in the room. This was the opening act for my meeting agenda that afternoon. "I want to play something for you," I told the group, feeling eerily calm but punchy, as I essentially called the meeting to what was about to be disorder. Our office walls were as thin as paper. I hit play, and the scene began. The music was blaring, and chants and cheers from the movie clip echoed through the office through the closed doors of my conference room.

My supervisors just sat there staring at the screen. I hadn't set the stage for why I was playing this. Honestly, I'm not sure what possessed me to tee this clip up myself. I could see on their faces they were bewildered. It had only been a few minutes, and then the door was flung open. "Kim, can I see you for a minute?" And with that, I was jerked out of this dystopian scene and beckoned back to reality.

Welcome to my weekly supervisor meeting.

Supervisors. The backbone of my business. I built my entire company around the patrol supervisor role. These officers roved the city in Clarion cars 24/7, handling all the issues that arose in the field. Training new employees. Delivering food. Checking uniforms. Providing bathroom breaks. Responding to emergencies. Holding posts down if someone called off. Finding someone to work the post if we had a call-off on the weekend. These were critical responsibilities, and I knew my employees would form a favorable or unfavorable impression of the company based not on their opinion of me but instead on their opinion of their immediate supervisor.

For a hands-on and controlling personality like mine, it was hard for me to entrust my company to the operations personnel from the top to the bottom. Regardless of who was on my operations team and their competence and capabilities, for years I tended to overrule and override the top-level managers. The supervisors reported to them, but I wanted to get front and center with my supervisors. It was not appropriate for the hierarchy, yet I just couldn't seem to help myself.

As written by Madell on the supervisors' impact on employee engagement, "The actions of an employee's direct supervisor have a crucial impact on employee engagement" (2023). And there is nothing more important to your company's performance than having an engaged workforce. As further discussed by Madell, "According to recruitment firm KeyStaff Inc., employee engagement is a key driver to increase productivity, innovation, retention, and competitive advantage" (2023).

I understood the direct impact my supervisors had on my people. I desperately needed the supervisors to perform their jobs well and take their roles seriously. We were growing so fast that I had lost my connections with many of the officers I had in the early years. If I didn't have the bandwidth to motivate individual employees, then I thought I needed to invest the time to motivate the supervisors to be a sufficient stand-in for me.

Early on, I mandated weekly supervisor meetings. It was a daunting task because we had to find a timeslot where our first, second, or third shifts could all come together to get briefed, coached, and instructed on the latest priorities. Because my patrol supervisors were the linchpin of the company, it was just too hard for me to back off their management and supervision. There were periods when I tried. I would turn over their meeting and let the operations manager run it. But oftentimes, I would insert myself into the meeting and "coach" up the team myself, much to the chagrin of my senior operations team.

The irony in the story is that I tended to ignore and discount my office management team to the priority of my field personnel. I was trampling on the entire management team's engagement by not allowing them to fully perform their duties, for better or for worse. But I wasn't seeing that at the time.

Becoming unhinged that one afternoon was years in the making.

MANAGEMENT 101

How could I have managed the operations hierarchy better? I wanted and needed my supervisors to be great first-line managers. Backing it up, I needed my senior operations team to be great managers of the supervisors. So that left me at the top of the pyramid. I needed to be a great manager of the senior operations team. But maybe I just didn't really want or know how to. I was being fearful and reactionary, alternating with being fearful and controlling, self-defeating, and demoralizing to my team. I just needed to have a well-defined system for how I could manage the middle managers taking the emotion out so it would have an effective ripple effect down the line.

Middle managers: Middle managers take the ideas and directives of top-level managers and ensure they are creatively, profitably, and punctually executed by lower-level managers. These middle-tier workers will straddle two critical parts of the pecking order: reporting to the top and overseeing the bottom. That was the missing element in my org chart.

But how to manage the middle managers? Here are four tips from MasterClass:

"Set clear metrics. Give managers clear metrics to set them up for success. These are best measured by establishing key performance indicators (KPIs) which will tell the managers what defines a job well done and can give them a roadmap toward

leading their team members. These KPIs are quantifiable goals and can help indicate which components of your business are the most beneficial to its progress, which ones can help optimize its performance, or which areas of your company may need work" (MasterClass 2022).

Had I set some KPIs, I would have keyed in a metric or two that measured both employee and client satisfaction. I needed engaged employees who performed their job well. That could have been measured qualitatively through employee survey responses or quantitively by the number of customer complaints, employee turnover, or percentage of open posts.

"Build relationships through check-ins. Check-ins are an effective way to build trust between managers and their higher-ups. These may be monthly or weekly and allow senior leadership to offer performance reviews and check in on progress" (MasterClass 2022).

This was a complete failure on my part. How could my middle managers communicate our ideas and directives to the supervisors if I wasn't meeting with my middle managers regularly to get us all aligned on the same page? I skipped this step completely to schedule the weeklies with the lower-level managers. Looking back, I wonder, if I had put that energy into weekly meetings with my middle managers, would we have been much more effective as a team?

"Know the required management skills. When hiring, be clear about the necessary competencies for the new management role. This will make for a smoother transition and a stronger management team" (MasterClass 2022).

Let's face it. Not everyone has natural people skills and is an effective manager. I look at myself and see my own deficiencies. My contention is this is one of the most overlooked deficiencies in organizations today. I should have spent time outlining the necessary competencies for success and training and building the skills in both myself and my team.

"Hire new managers with unique management styles. Higher-ups and mid-level managers do not have to have the same perspectives. Varying outlooks can help diversify efforts, encourage collaboration, and increase creativity" (MasterClass 2022).

Part of my fear was that middle managers did have different perspectives. I really just wanted them to manage things "my way." But if I had implemented the steps above this one, I could have allowed them to bring their own perspectives and better diversify my management team.

Part of my fear was allowing middle managers their own style.

On what planet would anyone think that "dyin' time" in the Thunderdome would be effective in motivating my team? I was clearly suffering from my own burnout, which was manifesting itself in the form of some extremely flawed thinking.

As written by Strauch and Bedosky, an "emotional meltdown" isn't exactly a medical diagnosis. "'It's used in popular discourse to describe when we are overcome emotionally, when we hit a breaking point,' says Robin Stern, PhD, licensed psychoanalyst and cofounder and director for the Yale Center for Emotional Intelligence in New Haven, Connecticut. "'For some people, a meltdown may look like crying uncontrollably. For others it may look like snapping at others or lashing out angrily. And for others it may involve panicking or running away from a stressful situation'" (2022).

I wasn't crying or running away. I was doubling down on the pressure of performance that I was feeling and trying to push that onto my supervisor team in some sort of crazy town illustration. There was little empowering left in me at all. Thankfully, I still had some reasonableness left and could listen to someone more clear-headed than me when that door opened that day.

The clip was pulled. No one ever commented, to me anyway, on that meeting. We moved along. But my foundation was starting to shift. A fracture will sometimes form a deep fissure or crevice in a rock. According to an article by the Queensland Government, fractures are commonly caused by stress exceeding the rock strength, causing the rock to lose cohesion along its weakest plane (2015).

I was climbing the mountain stepping on rocks that were splintering off into bits and pieces with every step. If I stepped wrong, they might give way completely, and the rocks and I would be tumbling down the mountain with no way back up. A rockslide. I didn't want it to be "dyin' time" for anyone, especially me. But I clearly wasn't all there mentally, and it was becoming a high-risk situation.

My team and I were all cracking, and I was the chief culprit. We just didn't quite realize it yet. Or maybe they saw me starting to crack and didn't know how to handle it. The crackle was in the air, indicating the fissure was expanding fast.

Under Pressure

"Kim, why don't you let me handle this issue?" my operations manager asked with a fatherly, somewhat patronizing look. "Our employees want to see the Kim they remember with a smile on her face." I waited for the other shoe to drop. "The Kim who is our leader and is positive and happy with an energy that is contagious."

Oh right. As opposed to the ball of stress I had constricted myself into, full of anxiety and angst wound tightly around the core. Leaking and dripping out as criticism and judgment as it bounced off my management team in various issues, crises, and problems. *Where did that happy girl go?* I hadn't seen her for quite some time. According to an article on WebMD:

> *When your body experiences a great amount of stress from your environment, there is a release of adrenaline. This release helps you focus so you can take on the situation. Adrenaline, also known as epinephrine, is a stress hormone. An adrenaline rush can feel like anxiousness, nervousness, or pure excitement as your body and mind are preparing for an event.*

> *The release of adrenaline helps increase your mental concentration. It doesn't take the pain away, rather it distracts you from the sensation of it. An adrenaline rush can heighten your abilities, making you feel invincible. This process is meant to help you overcome the situation that is causing your extreme stress (Bhandari 2022).*

Sounds like an amazing natural phenomenon known as "fight or flight," right? My body was helping me fight the good fight. I was pushing myself to my physical and emotional limits, and the adrenaline was keeping me functional. The problem was that I was seven years in on adrenaline, and I was turning brittle.

Far before I learned to run a company, I learned to bake. It was a skill handed down from my grandmothers. I loved to bake because I loved to eat, mostly sugar. In fact, I would be very content eating dessert for dinner. But of all the things I cooked and baked, I loved the challenge of making praline candy. The recipe required heating the mixture to a boil and cooking it to a perfect consistency. This is a finicky recipe, and it was a personal challenge to make it right with every batch.

I would pour the butter into the sugar mixture. This was the moment *most* critical in the process. The pralines called for the sugar and butter to get to the "soft ball" stage, a goopy concoction that stuck together when you dripped a few drips into the bowl of cold water. This was both an art and a science. Now they have a candy thermometer that takes all the thrill and personal challenge out of it. Who needs that when *I could try and figure it out myself?* That was my independent, stubborn self saying early on that I could figure this out on my own and have the personal satisfaction of getting it just right.

When I could roll the concoction together in the bowl of cold water for a few seconds, I knew I was ready for the next stage. It was time to stir my batter quickly and deliberately. But, from my many failed attempts prior, I knew there was a magical moment when it was ready to pour out onto the wax paper. If I didn't gauge the glossy thickness right and poured too early, then the pralines would just pool into liquid, lifeless circles that never set up. This had happened before, and I tried to scrape them back into the saucepan and stir it all back to the perfect consistency, but it was too little too late. I could tell if I had stirred the mixture too long; one stir too many, and the mix became too heavy, like molasses, and would barely pour out of my bowl. Once on the wax paper, my pralines would turn into thick blocks of sugar, hardened and brittle.

They had all the same amazing ingredients as the perfect creamy batch, but they had been hardened by one too many turns and became tough from the core to the edges. No one wanted candy like that. No one wanted to be around a person like that.

BURNOUT

"Thanks to the pioneering research of psychologist Christina Maslach and several collaborators, we know that burnout is a three-component syndrome that arises in response to chronic stressors on the job." As Monique Valcour continues to explain,

> *Stress is a fact of professional life, but extreme and unrelenting pressures can lead to the debilitating state of burnout. There are three primary symptoms—exhaustion, cynicism, and inefficacy.*
>
> ***Exhaustion*** *is the central symptom of burnout. It comprises profound physical, cognitive, and emotional fatigue that undermines people's ability to work effectively and feel positive about what they're doing. This can stem from the demands of an always-on, 24/7 organizational culture, intense time pressure, or simply having too much to do, especially when you lack control over your work, dislike it, or don't have the necessary skills to accomplish it.*
>
> ***Cynicism*** *represents a loss of engagement. It is a way of distancing yourself psychologically from your work. Instead of feeling invested in your assignments, projects, colleagues, customers, and other collaborators, you feel detached, negative, even callous. Cynicism can be the result of work overload, but it is also likely to occur in the presence of high conflict, unfairness, and lack of participation in decision making.*
>
> ***Inefficacy*** *refers to feelings of incompetence and a lack of achievement and productivity. People with this symptom of burnout feel their skills slipping and worry that they won't be able to succeed in certain situations or accomplish certain tasks. It often develops in tandem*

with exhaustion and cynicism because people can't perform at their peak when they're out of fuel and have lost their connection to work.

Research has linked burnout to many health problems, including hypertension, sleep disturbances, depression, and substance abuse. Moreover, it can ruin relationships and jeopardize career prospects (Valcour 2016).

I had allowed myself to be stirred into a severely overcooked batch running this company which was neither appealing nor edifying to anyone around me. I don't like to ask for help. I like to figure things out for myself and pride myself on the discipline of hard work and perseverance, which seems like a great mix of raw ingredients. But I didn't count on two significant intangibles along the way in this particular entrepreneurial journey.

ONE
We were on a shoestring budget, and I put too much responsibility onto my plate because I didn't want to spend any money for others to do it. On the organizational chart, I was the backup scheduler, backup payroll processor, backup supervisor, backup controller, backup security guard, and backup janitor. And when supervisors quit, or the scheduler walked out, or if I had to fire a key member of the management team, we were run so skinny that I was a permanent fixture on the backup plan. That may be fine when you have less than 100 employees. But five years later, with over 300 employees, my name was on too many primary and backup roles.

Let me rephrase that. Looking back, I put too much responsibility onto my plate because if someone couldn't do the job as the primary, I really only trusted myself as the backup. I put my name on the depth chart without thought of others who needed to be on there. Did I put too much stock on being the backup plan and too little on executing the primary plan? Did I think too little of my other team members, or too much of myself? It was probably a bit of both. But it was also reality. Security is a tough business. It was hard to attract and keep qualified people who didn't get burned out themselves with all the problems, the schedule, and the drama. And I had experienced the sting of some who had left quickly without adequate time to find their replacement. If they left me, then I would keep everything together, albeit at a personal cost. Because at the end of the day, I could always count on myself to rally through.

TWO

This business didn't sleep at night or on the weekends. So, therefore, neither did I. I would sleep with my phone underneath my pillow to take a crisis call at 1:00 a.m., or I would wake up at 3:00 a.m. and finish the payroll and then go back to sleep at 5:00 a.m. Saturday morning work turned into all day Saturday and eventually Sunday. The company completely absorbed all my time and energy, and my family got the scraps left over.

Did I have to take the calls? Handle the crises? Could someone else have taken on that role so that it didn't burn me to a crisp? Maybe so. But would they have cared as much? Maybe not. At that time, I wasn't ready to acquiesce my primary role to hope that the team would respond as I knew I always would. It was too important to me. We had to execute at the highest level possible, and I designated myself as the chief fixer of the problems.

Over time, repeated activation of the stress response takes a toll on the body. Research suggests that "chronic stress contributes to high blood pressure, promotes the formation of artery-clogging deposits, and causes brain changes that may contribute to anxiety, depression, and addiction" (Harvard Health Publishing 2020). More preliminary research suggests that "chronic stress may also contribute to obesity, both through direct mechanisms (causing people to eat more) or indirectly (decreasing sleep and exercise)" (Harvard Health Publishing 2020).

I was a walking, talking, classic case study of the effects of chronic stress and burnout. That's what my operations manager was trying to tell me that day. I had gained forty pounds, wasn't sleeping, was working eighty hours a week, and had become a brittle shell of my former self. But not only that, I was making poor decisions and lashing out at my employees. A prime example was the Thunderdome incident when I became unhinged (chapter eleven).

Looking back at that time, not only had my body borne the brunt of the stress, but my mental health was deteriorating. I had never exhibited any symptoms of depression prior to that time, but I started to wake up and feel like I was literally walking in quicksand and crying on a dime. I self-diagnosed with depression and made an appointment with my doctor.

"Do you want to try some medicine for depression?" he asked. It had only taken him a few minutes to assess I was a wreck. Through my tears, I just nodded my head. He handed me a script. "I'm going to give you some meds. Let's try this for thirty days."

On day two, I felt 1,000 percent better. I'm sure I had a cortisol imbalance. Who wouldn't after pushing themselves that hard for years on end?

The problem at that point was the damage was done. Just like that batch of brittle pralines, it was better to throw them in the trash and start over. How was I supposed to recover? How could happy-go-lucky Kim come back to life? I had boiled myself up over years and years of taking on too much responsibility that one person should never take. I put the company on my shoulders and broke my back in the process. Was it pride and ego that told me I could do it all? Perhaps.

But more than that, I wanted to prove to myself, my family, my friends, and the larger community that if I had been gifted the opportunity to run this company at the highest level, I wouldn't let anyone down. We had our family's financial future riding on it. I had employees facing life-and-death situations riding on it. I had clients counting on us. I didn't want to let anyone down. But in the end, running myself brittle caused everything to splinter down to the ground. I'm just grateful God allowed me not to succumb to that stress by causing a permanent end to my story and that I did eventually find a path to rejuvenation and recovery.

From my perspective as a woman CEO and business owner, I see the pressures that come from being in a role that is generally more male-dominated. I believe when women have the opportunity to perform at the highest level, we don't want to let anyone down. Or we want to prove we are just as capable, or more capable, as a man of doing the same job. Women put the most pressure on ourselves than any other person could every lay on us. But then we put ourselves at risk for the stress that accompanies that expectation.

Any business owner or CEO, male or female, also faces the immense pressure and stress that come from the responsibilities of the position. My team members saw it in my changed behavior, but I didn't allow myself any perspective to analyze how my suffering was burning me up. Sometimes help needs to come from an outside source, whether it's a therapist, advisory board member, family member, or employee. And we need to be open to asking for it and have the open-mindedness to hear it. It's important not to let the stress drown out the alert.

Unfortunately, if we don't get the cues and messaging from one of those external sources, the alert may come from within and signal some part of our body that change needs to happen. Because the body does keep score, and it won't stay silent forever.

If you are experiencing burnout, it's important to take a pause and approach the situation from a high level. Ask yourself the following questions:

1. What can I do to make a change in my personal self-care to be healthier? It may just be pausing to take deep breaths, walking outside, or not looking at emails at night or booking some margin in your schedule for something that brings you joy.
2. Who can I ask for help? It may be someone at work who can take some of the load. Or it may be someone who can help manage your personal life and family obligations to allow you to navigate the demands of a professional life in an intense period.
3. What can I change in the stressful environment in which I'm operating? And if nothing comes to mind, then what can I change in my mindset not to succumb to the pressure?
4. How can I recharge myself and get back to equilibrium in order to be effective in my position?

If someone is experiencing intense chronic stress, when the adrenaline wears off, the pain bubbles back to the surface. Just as our company was beginning to come into a season of great accolades and recognition for what we had accomplished, the Clarion team was continuing to brittle and break on all sides. And I'm sure, although I felt I had the best intentions, I was a key ingredient in the mix that was churning and burning us all up.

Personality, Pressure, and Predicaments

"No wonder you're so stressed out," my therapist said laughing while looking down at my personality test scores. "According to your Enneagram scores, your two main personality types are a perfectionist (one) and a peacemaker (nine). That combination means you hold yourself and others to the highest standards but avoid conflict, so you just take everything on yourself."

I wasn't laughing. I was sitting in front of her because I had a problem I hadn't verbalized to anyone, and I knew I needed professional help to solve it. I was dangerously close to the edge, mentally and physically. The tipoff for me was the scary thoughts running around my head in recent mornings. *It's okay if you have a heart attack or stroke out and die. You've made it. The company is financially sound and profitable. The kids are basically grown. Everyone will be sad, but they will all be okay.*

Those thoughts scared me into taking action. I had met a therapist a few years earlier at a church conference and asked her to speak at one of my NAWBO (National Association of Women Business Owners) luncheon events. The topic I chose for her was "Burnout remedies for high-achieving women." Well, here I was, the classic case, sitting in her office so that she could diagnose and help fix me.

PERSONALITY

According to 16Personalities, "There are various theories of personality development, but most theories agree that the personality is developed in early childhood and consists of the following three influences: heredity, environment, and situations" (16Personalities 2023). A combination of both nature and nurture, I wasn't going to change my personality that was formed forty years prior. But in my professional life, I found out that pushing my natural personality into a significant leadership role in a challenging industry had accelerated the stress level and consequent burnout.

MYERS-BRIGG

I find personality tests fascinating and have taken various tests before. First was the Myers-Brigg personality test. This was the classic test that has been used for years in business settings. The first time I took it was in my organizational behavior class at SMU when I was enrolled in the executive MBA program. There were about fifty of us in our cohort. We took the test, and then the professor sorted us according to our scores. Only two of us scored the personality of a "Defender" (or ISFJ). "This personality type carries the traits of being: Introverted, Sensing (observing), Feeling, and Judging" (16Personalities 2023).

THE DEFENDER

"The ISFJ is driven by personal values, is conscientious, a hard worker that values relationships and strives to cooperate and maintain harmony with others. For Defenders, 'good enough' is rarely good enough. People with this personality type can be meticulous to the point of perfectionism. They take their responsibilities personally, consistently going above and beyond and doing everything that they can to exceed others' expectations" (16Personalities 2023).

And just to prove personalities don't change, I would be described almost identically twenty-five years later in a completely different personality test format.

Where were the other forty-eight in the class that day? Turns out the majority were clumped together in what were considered more "CEO" type personalities. The biggest group consisted of those with the combination of personality traits that are most likened to CEO success, nicknamed "the Commander" (Johns 2018).

THE COMMANDER

"ENTJs (Commanders) are assertive, resilient, and goal-oriented people eager to take charge in just about any situation. Bold and strategic, they're confident in their ability to overcome challenges and don't waste time on trivial details. As big picture thinkers and visionaries, ENTJs are innovative and make excellent leaders (MyPersonality 2023).

"Since ENTJs are quick-witted, they are decisive and solve problems quickly yet effectively. They aren't afraid of taking calculated risks, which is one of the reasons why many Commanders are drawn to entrepreneurship. As leaders, they're great at managing people, delegating tasks, and streamlining processes to maximize results and efficiency" (MyPersonality 2023).

So did that mean with my personality that I wouldn't be as successful? Not at all. As Johns explains, "Other personality types can still be excellent CEOs, but introverted people may become exhausted by the exposure to the limelight. In contrast, extroverts are energized by human interaction. ENTJs also have the advantage of quickly acting on intuition and using rationality in decision-making. These skills give them confidence and keep them from second-guessing every decision they make" (Johns 2018).

And that was true of me. I agonized over decisions. It's what is called "overthinking." Most often for me, this happened during the wee hours of the morning, wringing my thoughts over and over again. That stemmed from my natural personality. I am a "feeler" and not a "thinker."

As the Myers & Briggs Foundation clarifies, these two statements describe the different decision-making factors:

THINKING

"When I make a decision, I like to find the basic truth or principle to be applied, regardless of the specific situation involved. I like to analyze pros and cons, and then be consistent and logical in deciding. I try to be impersonal, so I won't let my personal wishes—or other people's wishes—influence me" (The Myers & Briggs Foundation 2023).

FEELING

"I believe I can make the best decisions by weighing what people care about and the points-of-view of persons involved in a situation. I am concerned with values and what is the best for the people involved. I like to do whatever will establish or maintain harmony. In my relationships, I appear caring, warm, and tactful" (The Myers & Briggs Foundation 2023).

But the Myers & Briggs Foundation cautions not to confuse feeling with emotion. "Everyone has emotions about the decisions they make." And also not to confuse thinking with intelligence. "It's just that one puts more weight on objective principles and impersonal facts (Thinking) and the other puts more weight on personal concerns and the people involved (Feeling)" (The Myers & Briggs Foundation 2023).

I had a lot of people to consider in my entrepreneurial journey. And, after time, I began feeling swamped by the considerations of all involved. Strapping all those customers and employees onto my pack and trying to pull it myself just caused me to dig myself a little deeper into the dirt every year.

DISC ASSESSMENT

A few years into running my company, I became intrigued with the DiSC assessment. A DiSC assessment is a behavioral assessment that businesses and other organizations sometimes use to determine employees' and managers' leadership strengths and weaknesses.

"DiSC is an acronym that stands for the four main personality profiles described in the DiSC model: (D)ominance, (i)nfluence, (S)teadiness and (C)onscientiousness" (Discprofile 2023).

"People with D personalities tend to be confident and place an emphasis on accomplishing bottom-line results.

"People with i personalities tend to be more open and place an emphasis on relationships and influencing or persuading others.

"People with S personalities tend to be dependable and place the emphasis on cooperation and sincerity.

"People with C personalities tend to place the emphasis on quality, accuracy, expertise, and competency" (Discprofile 2023).

The test had been a recommendation from a business coach. I hired him a few years into our business to assist with some management and leadership topics as well as to hold me accountable for implementing best practice strategies. I'm all about leveraging help from subject matter experts. Mentors, advisors, peers, and coaches can all help contribute to a leader's growth personally and professionally. It was his idea to assess me and my team to see how our natural personality dynamics were a fit with the demands of each of our working positions.

My business coach looked at my scores and then turned to me with a look of concern. "Kim, the bigger the disparity between your natural personality and the role you are performing, the higher the stress level." I already knew my natural scores. Lower than 50 percent for "drive" and "influence," and very much above 50 percent for "steadiness" and "conscientious." It coincided with my Myers-Briggs results. He went on, "Because of your position in the company and the massive interpersonal requirements, you are performing in high ranges for both dominance (drive) and influence."

Again, very telling. Driving results and managing an employee-heavy service-based business were straining me against my natural personality strengths. As I pulled that pack, the tension began to show. But this time, though sweaty and exhausted, I kept on pushing, using all my strength to forge ahead, carrying this impossibly heavy pack. So much that it had driven me into the therapist's office. A coach was one thing. But now I needed a mental health professional. I was concerned I was about to just drop in the road, unable to go an inch more.

ENNEAGRAM PERSONALITY TEST

As described by Jennifer Nied,

> The Enneagram is a personality typing tool (à la Myers-Briggs) that distills your behaviors, thinking patterns, and feelings into a numerical "type." According to Ginger Lapid-Bogda, PhD, "The goal of the test is to deliver a better understanding of your motivations, strengths, and weaknesses or 'what your fears are.'"
>
> The Enneagram does this by giving you a "type" or number one through nine, which is placed on a nine-point circular diagram. Each of the "types" is spread around the edge of the circle and connected to one another via diagonal lines. Not only does the test determine your numerical type, but it also connects you to other types within the circle, helping to explain how your personality may shift under different scenarios (Nied 2022).

What I became fascinated with was the fact that personalities can be nuanced and changed with a person's mental health. It wasn't so much that a perfectionist and a peacemaker couldn't be a competent CEO; instead, it was that I had allowed myself to succumb to pressure and duress that was causing me to make unhealthy choices for myself and affecting the interpersonal relationships surrounding me based on my natural personality tendencies.

Then, the voices in my head started talking and causing me angst. *Why couldn't I have a better personality mix?* Of course, there's no "wrong" personality, but it felt that way to me. *A peacemaker seems nice, but a perfectionist?* I didn't like that label. And apparently, the combination of the two had sent me into a spiraling pit of maladaptive behaviors that was backfiring. I was digging myself a Clarion grave with my natural personality tendencies.

After that download from the therapist, I needed to figure some things out for myself. In order to get a remedy for the issue, it was time to dig into the Enneagram descriptors for the labels. And Molly Owens had some captivating descriptions:

One - Perfectionist.

"Core Motivation: Perfectionists (Ones) strive to be good and honorable—and to live a life with purpose. They seek the best and most correct way to do things" (Owens 2021).

Okay. I was totally fine with that assessment. Things were looking up. Maybe this personality wasn't so "bad."

"Deepest Fear: Perfectionists (Ones) fear being "bad people," morally flawed, or otherwise seen as imperfect. They cope with this fear by being rigidly disciplined and very hard on themselves (and often, those around them, too)" (Owens 2021).

Hmmm. Well, this one was difficult to read. Not only was I my own worst critic, but it explained why I was getting crossways with my people. Fear was completely driving my behavior. As a matter of fact, the whole company had been built on my platform of fear. Fear that we wouldn't make it financially. Fear that something major would happen to one of my guards. Fear that a major crime would happen to one of our clients on our watch.

How in the world was I going to remedy this situation? I wanted to get to the healthy part of my personality and push away from the fear. It would take the next few years to really dig into the growth in my personality, but as an immediate takeaway, I decided that I needed to shift my mindset. The first person I needed to stop being so hard on was myself. I had to give myself some room to fail.

I understood my personality type is a natural workaholic. There was clearly a work/life imbalance that I needed to resolve. But more than that, I told myself it would be okay if Clarion Security operated at less than an "A+." That there could be some mistakes we could make and still be a strong, successful company. In my mind, if I could lower the required standard from perfect, then I wouldn't be such a harsh critic toward my inner self and drive myself in unreasonable ways.

I chose to get help when I was at an extremely low point, which would be my hope for anyone who finds themselves in an unhealthy relationship, role, or environment. Sometimes it takes a professional third party to show us how to get unstuck and move us into a better place to be a better leader, partner, parent, or friend.

According to Meghan Mannarino, "If you feel paralyzed by stress, can't control your emotions or depression interferes with your ability to function, then it may be time to seek professional care. It's not a sign of weakness. Your body is probably sending out alerts already that it's time to take better care of your mental health" (2023).

As you assess your stress level, burnout factor, and the possible need for professional help, I recommend the following:

- Take any one of the personality tests I mentioned to get a baseline assessment of how your natural personality aligns with the specific demands of your career. I believe the Enneagram is more nuanced and provides more takeaways than the other two, but any of them can provide a baseline. Then be aware and assess the stress it takes to perform your role. If there is a disconnect between your natural personality traits and the demands of your specific position, know you are going to have to manage that stress proactively so it doesn't overwhelm you and lead to burnout.
- Put together an action plan when you start experiencing burnout symptoms, as I outlined in the prior chapter. Rate yourself from one to ten on each category, and then write down an action plan. The hope is that you can implement some strategies to come back to center mentally in an organic manner and that you can recover by making some tangible and specific action items to refresh and reinvigorate you in your career as well as your emotional stability.
- Acknowledge if you've pushed yourself to a breaking point, if the burnout scale is raging and impacting your physical and/or mental health in a dangerous manner, and if you don't know how to recover. It's not a sign of weakness to get help. It's the smartest decision you can make.

I waited almost too late. And even then, it would take some drastic measures to finally get back to center, physically and mentally. But before I could get there, I would shortly live out the consequences of ignoring the intense burnout and chronic stress.

But what about my team?

They were operating in the same difficult environment with a leader driving and pushing for results and perfection. How were they doing?

And, because I needed to pause to focus on navigating my own treacherous path in that moment, I didn't see the storm clouds bearing down on me that were about to roll in quickly and consequentially.

Ransomed

It was December 2017. The condominium was booked, and the trip was planned. Friends and family— coming together for the last week of the year to celebrate a successful and profitable year. Taking a pause from work, finally, to enjoy a long overdue vacation. A break to prioritize family over the company. How could I have known the small fortune we paid for the ski chalet would be a mere pittance once I realized the true cost of this trip, both personally and professionally?

Let me put this story in perspective...

I was so consumed by the flickering flames of my personal burnout that I didn't notice the burning embers simmering all across my management team. We were all pushing so hard. I was the lead horse tethered with my key team members driving with all our might in an all-out sweat to keep achieving business milestones. We were in our fourth year, driving sales up exponentially higher than the year before. More clients meant more employees. Sometimes we would sign up a client who had just experienced a security incident. And because of that, time was of the essence. Their property was vulnerable. If we could deliver a quick, almost immediate response, the business was ours. It was a differentiator to be that nimble, and we knew it. This meant we needed to hire people quickly. Lots of them.

Push, push, push.

We were growing so fast; my managers and I couldn't keep up. We each rotated being managers on duty every weekend, but we were never really off. There were too many client and employee issues happening around the clock. Until the stress broke us down one way or another, that is.

At that point, I was no good to anyone on my team. I didn't know how broken down I was. I could only hope that by outworking everyone on the team, that could motivate them to keep going. And so, we continued at breakneck speed the rest of that year until the last week of the year with a short respite on my schedule.

We arrived at our beautifully appointed lodge. It was a tranquil night. Snow on the ground, not too cold, stars dotting the sky illuminating our path. Everyone was in a celebratory mood heading down the street to where the rest of the group was gathered. The party was in full gear. My phone rang. It was the supervisor on duty. "This is Kim," I answered as I stepped out of the path of the lively chatter to get the update. It was bad. "Ms. Kim, Robert quit. He called me just now. He said he left all his company equipment on the table and walked out."

I was disappointed but not shocked. He'd been with me for many years and was integral to the operation in many ways. As smart and capable a manager as he was, I had seen him react with a quick fuse emotionally to situations in the past. He was experiencing stress in his personal life. And that just added to all the stress we were all operating under day in and out. What caused him to walk out like that? I'm not sure. It may have been personal or business, or maybe both. "Thanks for letting me know," I answered. Determined not to let work interfere with my long-planned vacation, I walked back into the party and rejoined the revelry.

Two hours later, the calls started again in rapid succession:

- "Ms. Kim, the clock-in system is not working."
- "Ms. Kim, sorry to bother you, but no one can get on the system to see their schedules. And when they call to clock in, the phone just rings."

Well, now the party was over for me. Something was wrong. I left the merriment and walked back to the condo to retrieve my computer and reboot the scheduling system. And when I did, there it was: a box right in the middle of the screen, flashing the following message: "Your system has been shut down. Here's the address to send us Bitcoin to get it back."

I was in disbelief. I never had anything happen like this before. Four hundred and fifty employees with no online access to the schedules. Employees who couldn't clock in or out, which would impact their pay if we didn't get this sorted out quickly. As of that very moment, our entire company was shut down. And it was the New Year's Eve holiday weekend. My options were limited.

My disappointment led to discouragement, then to resignation. This was now a work trip for me. It wasn't the first time work would crater into my personal life, and I shouldered the task at hand. The solution was to rebuild the scheduling system while my family enjoyed the remainder of the ski trip. And ultimately, with cybersecurity insurance, the entire situation was remedied in a few weeks' time.

Once I caught my breath from the disaster, I started to do some research. This was a third-party proprietary scheduling software. How did the hackers know I had that particular vendor? It wasn't like a mainstream system. I didn't have a main network or server in my office. This was a remote server that was set up. It didn't have any sensitive information in it, like addresses or social security numbers. Then, it dawned on me—there were only two other people who knew the password to that system, and one was Robert. This happened two hours after he quit. Could he have sold that password to the dark web?

I could never prove this theory, but the timing did not seem coincidental. And research seemed to corroborate my gut intuition. According to an article from the blog *ID Agent*, "Malicious insider risk is an unpleasant but ongoing situation that every business has to deal with daily. Both current and former employees can intentionally damage a company, and just one disgruntled employee can wreak havoc fast. However it happens, malicious insider actions are responsible for an estimated 25 percent of confirmed data breaches. They're also risks for ransomware deployment, credential compromise, and more nightmare scenarios. Exploring the ways that malicious insiders can shed light on why an employee might become a malicious insider" (2022).

There are myriad ways for an employee to do damage. Unhappy former employees can damage their employers when they leave by stealing data or proprietary information. According to a report by Gigamon, "35 percent of all ransomware attacks were caused by a malicious insider. Current employees who need money or feel slighted in some way can do nasty things like selling their credentials on the dark web. Malicious actors can also directly unleash a cyberattack by deploying malware themselves" (ID Agent 2022).

Maybe he did, maybe he didn't. But if he did, then that would mean he was disgruntled and unhappy. The bigger question was, *What got him to that point, and could there have been anything to prevent it?* Then I switched to my current concern. *How many of my team members were sitting in their seats feeling the same way and were slowly but surely disengaging?*

EMPLOYEE BURNOUT

I realized I had a bigger problem than a hack on my scheduling system. My key employees were succumbing to burnout. Not only were they working for a high-growth company in a high-stress industry, but their leader was also constantly pushing them. I'm sure my pushing (or control) of the team came across as critical in their eyes. They say that one negative statement can nullify dozens of positive statements. I was part of the problem, not the solution.

In an article from *Forbes* titled "Managers, Here Are Three Warning Signs Your Employees Are Burnt Out," Heidi Lynne Kurter states, "The worst thing a manager can do is turn a blind eye to employee burnout. It's not until it's too late that managers realize the severity of it. At this point, it's nearly impossible to reverse it and managers would rather write off the employee than put in the effort to re-engage them. As such, burnt-out employees end up parting ways with the company.... When employees are unhappy, it's hard to ignore. Their negative emotions manifest through cynicism and irritability toward clients, coworkers, and even their manager. Whether positive or negative, emotions are contagious and will impact the team which spreads throughout the company" (Kurter 2021).

So what are the leading causes of employee burnout? They include,

- "Unclear expectations
- "Poor communication
- "Being overworked and underappreciated
- "Feeling the need to be constantly connected to work
- "Working in a toxic environment
- "Lack of support from a manager and/or coworkers
- "Being micromanaged" (Kurter 2021)

I missed the warning signs. Or I saw them and ignored them. And it was costly on both sides. If I had just taken the time to at least air out some of his frustration and let him vent, perhaps this would not have ended that way. Or at all. I thought he knew I respected him for his work and that I did care, but now I see that might have been all in my head. There wasn't enough interaction and enough positive communication to remedy the situation.

And there were things I would have done differently before my team succumbed to burnout, which caused other key members to leave over the years. As described by David Smart, "It's important to ward off burnout on your team as well: Insist on time for rest and renewal, set realistic work limits, boost your team's sense of control, provide meaningful recognition, and ask people what help or training they need to succeed" (Smart 2021).

Unfortunately, at this point, many of my key management employees had probably already hit burnout mode. So could I have attempted to reengage the employees?

In that same article, Kurter continues, "Managers need to own up to their role in creating workplace stress so they can prevent it from continuing. To start, managers should meet with their employees consistently on a one-on-one basis to check in with where they're at mentally as well as professionally. The key is to actively listen and be receptive rather than dismiss their complaints or negative feedback. The worst thing a manager can do is become defensive or blame the employee when they open up about their stressors. Managers should prioritize finding a solution that will not only support the employee but also help relieve some of their workload. If they're unable to do so, they need to be honest with the employee instead of giving them false hope or leaving them wondering" (Kurter 2021).

But, in order to fix the issues with my team, I had to focus on myself first, as I was in pretty bad shape. The leader sets the tone, models the behavior, and owns the response. As illustrated in the article "Leaders: Put Your Own Oxygen Mask On First," written by Daphna Horowitz, "By practicing self-care, you're also modeling this behavior for those around you. We don't always take the time to invest in ourselves, especially when times are tough and time is in short supply. Just like we need to take care of ourselves to be in top form, our team needs to take care of themselves too. But how will our people know that looking after themselves is a priority if we don't role model it?" (Horowitz 2020).

A leader with integrity takes the accolades and also takes the blame. I knew it had been hard being on my team, knowing I had such high expectations for the company. I could have done a much better job supporting each of them as we climbed up and up and up. When you are scaling the mountain, a strong leader stays behind, makes sure everyone makes it up, and only then do they follow as the very last one up the hill. I had been racing up the hill and then, from the top, shouting down, "Come on up. It's fine. You can make it!" And if one faltered, I wasn't there to help them get back to center. Either they made it, or they didn't. And if they did, be it of their own accord or with another fellow climber, it wasn't because I stopped to help them up. I was ahead and leading but also trying to put the train tracks down ahead of my employees. No matter what shape those tracks happened to be.

So how could I have supported them better? My number one takeaway would be to have more availability to show my team

I had time to listen. It's so simple and basic. Had I scheduled a one-on-one with each of my management team even once a month and asked some open-ended questions, I bet we could have come to some resolutions together. It's about being intentional. While being caught up in the whirlwind of growth and crisis management, I didn't realize I had been taking them all for granted. I was not letting them know by word and action that I cared, even if I couldn't alleviate the stress of each of their respective positions.

When you are the one at the top of the organizational chart, your team isn't going to come to you. Don't let busyness drown out the importance of checking in on your employees. They just need you to open the proverbial door to let them in. Have the courage to ask each one of them, "What could I do better to support you in your position?"

It would be one of the biggest life lessons I took from my entrepreneurial journey. At the end of the day, you can have a successful company on paper measured by dollars and cents, but the way you treat people and choose to build a positive, inspiring, and encouraging dynamic with your team is what has a real, lasting impact.

What was the ultimate cost of the trip? The time lost with my family? A further stressor to my mental health? A lost key employee? A Bitcoin ransom? They were all adding up to a deficit that was starting to feel insurmountable. As I sat there in the ski chalet hunched over my computer, looking out at the beautiful snow-covered mountain repairing my scheduling system, it felt as if I was stuck in a cave looking at a world that was living without me in it. And that's what was happening. I wasn't engaging in my life anymore. I was losing. But my company was winning. And winning big.

PART 4

GAINING TRACTION ALL THE WAY TO THE TOP

Winning Memphis Style

"If you want to have a chance to win this contract, you are going to have to partner together, be competitive, and present a proposal compelling enough for the Shelby County commissioners to vote for you." The head of a non-profit tasked with promoting women and minority business opportunity was preaching to the room with the charisma and energy that defined his personality. And we sat there just staring back at him as his voice crackled with electricity. Everyone in the audience was drinking it in, heady with the possibilities we hadn't considered before today's meeting. "In your presentation, you need to feature how you can deliver your service on a level equal to or better than the existing provider."

It wasn't just any contract he was talking about. It was *the* contract. The biggest municipal contract in the city. A multi-million-dollar armed guard contract for all the Shelby county government buildings, including the jail and the courts. Fifty-plus guards working in five buildings across the city of Memphis. And the company we would potentially be unseating wasn't just any company—it was *the* largest security guard company in the world. A $15 billion revenue company that had been the incumbent security provider for the past ten years. This was a tall, tall order for any company going after the contract. Much less our group of mostly micro security guard companies.

Could we really do it?

Walking into the meeting that day, none of us thought we could. We had been invited together by the head of a nonprofit that had as its mission a goal to provide resources to help scale women- and minority-owned businesses and assist them in bidding and winning municipal and corporate business. We were invited because we were all active members of this organization that had pledged to help us.

I looked around and was impressed at how he had galvanized the troops. There were fifteen different firms. Fourteen of them were minority African American businesses, mostly small in organization and size. As we went around and introduced our companies, I knew some of the names from prior bidding opportunities but didn't recognize many faces. There were a couple of women scattered throughout, but I was the only Caucasian in the room. After his speech, we were presented with the first call to action.

"I think you guys need to elect a leader from the companies in the room. Then once you have your leader, you can brainstorm on how you could work together on a collaborative bid." I noted that I was the biggest company in the room and had the best chance of leading a competitive proposal, so I stood up and asked for the lead role from my peers.

"In order for our proposal to be seriously considered, we need to instill confidence in the commissioners that we can perform on the contract. My company has the resources and résumé to be considered a legitimate contender. I have a solid track record of performance with the city of Memphis. And I have current armed-guard contracts, so the prior performance is there." All true and important. But I agreed with the pitch we had just heard and needed to say it. "I could compete for this contract on a standalone basis, but I believe by coming together with other small and minority-owned businesses, we present a compelling case for the county government that is trailblazing." And with that, I was voted in as the de facto leader.

THE WINNING STRATEGY
The words kept ringing in my ear. "We have to be competitive in order to unseat the incumbent." And being competitive meant we had to underbid the current provider. That was the reality, and I knew it. Having an equal or higher bid would never get us in the door. We were the major underdog. I would need to hold current salaries on the contract steady, propose a bill rate less than the current provider, and cut down my margin some in order to win the bid. I'd done it before. I just had never done it on this scale.

Not all the companies in the room were willing to be that aggressive. I pitched the strategy for the next hour. Some companies weren't interested in bidding at all. Some wanted higher pay rates and didn't agree with my strategy. At the end of the meeting, there were four other African-American companies willing to partner with me. We made a verbal agreement on the pricing structure and partnership allocations, in which I agreed to be the prime contractor and allowed my new partners to take a significant portion of the business if we won. I was both humbled and energized by the chance to appeal to the Shelby County Commissioners now. As a coalition of local women- and minority-owned security guard companies that chose to work together, we were an embodiment of the demographics of Memphis and the spirit of true local entrepreneurship. We had our team, and it was a compelling one.

We could have a chance. I left that day with a glimmer of hope. It was a possibility. But I knew it would take all we could give to be considered. We were all a bit giddy, adjourning for the afternoon. My new business partners and I had no idea just how hard the journey on this trail would really be. In that moment, we were fresh-faced and energized. Onward and upward we went.

THE BOUT BEGINS

We put together our proposal in the following months, finalized the cost, and submitted it. It's all public record, so we would know the results immediately. The strategy seemed to work. We were the low bid. It was the beginning of June, and the contract started on July 1. We won, right? If only it had been that easy. We needed a majority vote from the Shelby County Commission to get official approval. And so, the public ratifying process began. And it turned into a boxing match for which none of us were sufficiently prepared.

SHELBY COUNTY COMMISSION

As stated on the official Shelby County, Tennessee, website, "The Shelby County Commission consists of thirteen Shelby County Commissioners. Each commissioner serves in Single Member Districts 1–13. Districts are assigned representatives based on the district's population, and each commissioner serves their district on the same level. The motion to approve our contract required a majority vote of the Commissioners present. Abstain and recusal votes have no bearing in calculating if an item passes or fails… Committee and Commission meetings are open to the public. The public is welcome to attend meetings and may speak on any agenda item by completing and submitting a Request to Speak Card" (2023).

In retrospect, we should have known better than to expect a rubber stamp from the commission. The incumbent was politically savvy, with deep pockets and an abundance of legal resources. And probably had strong relationships with the county from having the account for many years. The heavyweight.

Our coalition of companies and I were new to the scene, presenting an alternative solution as the hometown heroes, championing the cause for local minority- and women-owned businesses across town. We were untested and unproven. The featherweight.

ROUND ONE

"This meeting is called to order. We have a quorum on hand." said the speaker at the public commissioner meeting. And then, after a while, we were up. I heard, "Next on the agenda is the contract for armed guard security." We were on the card. Heavyweight versus featherweight. Looking back, the moderator should have just said to us, "Are. You. Ready. To. Rumble…?" but it wouldn't have mattered because, within minutes, we were trying to catch our breath in full knock-down mode. It came from a one-two combo from the current employees under the contract, then the incumbent. I was left reeling, waiting for the bell, so I could digest what had just happened.

It must have been carefully orchestrated by the opponent. "Before we vote, we will hear from the public." And the first person who filled out the Request to Speak Card walked to the front of the room—a current employee on the contract. "Yes, thank you," he said, wearing the current company's uniform. "If you vote for this new company, we've found out they will be reducing our salaries. And not giving us adequate benefits." He went on to elaborate, but essentially the gist was that if the employees remained on the contract and stayed with our company, they would suffer financially. I could sense that the commissioners found this very concerning because they then asked many follow-up questions. There were a multitude of current employees in the room, with several speaking on the theme. They had strength in numbers.

ROUND TWO

It was time for the next topic. Up to speak was an executive from the current security guard company. And it turned personal. "The person who owns Clarion Security, Mrs. Heathcott, has no significant experience at all. This is one of the highest profile armed guard contracts in Shelby county."

He went on, "She won't be able to handle it, and it is a big risk for the commissioners to consider giving such a weighty contract to her company." There was more—but it was more of the same.

It was a PR nightmare, full of inaccuracy and innuendo, to which I had no response. I hadn't prepared a defense. Thankfully, they called the match for the night. Voting was tabled. We were asked to come back and explain the salary and benefits at the next meeting. But how to recover from the damage invoked on my leadership capabilities?

LOSING

We were barely alive. Rounds had ticked off, and things hadn't gotten much better. Instead, time had become my enemy. We kept presenting the merits of our proposal and answering questions. Presenting our benefits. Advocating for our experience. This went on for several weeks, but the vote kept getting tabled. And I was running out of time. I had to hire forty-six officers to be able to staff the contract that would start July 1. The best option was to have the existing personnel come to my office, fill out applications, and get hired. And the majority of them weren't showing up. I was doing my best to staff the positions with existing personnel, but we were running low on armed guards.

We ran the numbers at the office. Somewhat desperate, with my voice tinged with anxiety, I tallied the count and relayed it to my HR team, "We need ten more people." It was one week prior to the takeover. The current employees on the account were deliberately not coming over to fill out applications, even though we had implored them several times in person. I think they were hoping I would fail and have to tell the county I couldn't staff the job. And I still didn't have the votes from the commissioners. My time was up. There was one more commissioner meeting before the July 1 deadline, four days prior to the contract start. I was at round ten. My adversary knew I was on the ropes. It was now or never.

ROUND TEN

I had to come fighting from my corner with a winning strategy:

- First, I decided I couldn't ask the existing officers to take a pay cut. They would already be losing out on some vacation benefits by leaving the other firm and being hired by Clarion. I would just have to take a margin hit. So, I decided to raise my pay rate slightly above what they were making currently.
- Second, I needed a visible advocate in front of the commissioners. I asked my operations manager to make a public show of support and pull a speaker card. I also asked my subcontractors to speak as well.
- Third, I presented a side-by-side comparison of our benefits, and we matched everything they had with the current provider. I had satisfied the commission's request to ensure my new employees would have comparable benefits if they came to work for me.

And then, the bell rang. It was showtime. From the audience, I could see movement and lots of sidebar conversations from the commissioners attending. Then some of the commissioners started disappearing behind closed doors. I started to panic. *Were they recusing themselves to not materialize at the vote, thereby dooming our bid?* And then, it was time for my ops manager to speak on our behalf. He walked up to the podium. I knew he didn't want to talk, but I appreciated that he did anyway. "I believe in this company and our ability to handle the contract." He was authoritative and presented well. I may have been the only one in the room who noticed he didn't give me a personal vote of confidence as I had asked. But it didn't matter. We had all done enough.

The scores were tallied. We got the majority vote, five days before the contract started. And because we won the vote, the next day the phone started ringing. All the employees on the current job wanted to know when they could come to our office to submit their applications. We would make our numbers.

GO TIME
We did it.

It was a busy Monday morning in July, and the conveyor belts were rolling. The courts were open for business, and the metal detectors were on and rolling. Our guards were deployed over five buildings and twenty-three stations across the city of Memphis and Shelby county, scanning the mass of people in lines headed in for their day at court, jail, or various and sundry Shelby county businesses. Our security officers were outfitted in their charcoal gray Class A uniforms with the orange Clarion patch, armed with Sig P226 handguns that sat in Level III holsters. As soon as we got the vote, I went and bought sixty firearms from a local gun store and ordered every available holster on Amazon, and then handed them out within forty-eight hours over the weekend. We were manned on every post, looking sharp *and* doing our job to secure all the county government buildings in the city.

Sometimes winning in business with a significant victory is just a vicious fight, especially if you are an underdog. You could be fighting an opponent with unfair tactics. And you might feel like you are losing, and it's hopeless. But then one tiny break happens, momentum shifts slightly, and you get back on your feet because it's not over. But a fight will definitely be over if you give up and call it quits.

I was in a fight against the $15 billion behemoth security company that had the contract for the previous ten years. A fight against their employees who didn't want to work for Clarion. A fight against the perception that a woman who *didn't* have a military, armed service, or law enforcement background could properly run a company that could handle an armed contract of that magnitude and significance. A fight against time that I couldn't pull together in just four days.

Why didn't I succumb to the pressure and throw in the towel? Because of how hard I had to fight just to get to that July morning. It wasn't just those four days prior to the contract when we were scrambling like mad to make the deadline. It was seven years filled with operational issues, personnel issues, and personal struggles. Holidays, nights, and weekends with no breaks. Sacrificing time with my family to keep the wheels of the company turning. Being swallowed up in the chaos of fast-paced growth, which caused me to ignore my personal health and well-being. We were on the brink of a significant victory that would cement our reputation in the market and be one of our top contracts. I would *not* fold, and I could *not* give up even if things sometimes seemed insurmountable.

There's *always* a way up the mountain. It may take every ounce of stamina that you have or longer than you think. Don't give up. And mark the trail as you head toward the top for others who come behind you. I was trying to do the right thing. It was a huge win for local Memphis companies, for women and minority business owners. Why did it have to be so hard for our bid? Maybe so it would be easier for the next group of small, minority- and women-owned businesses.

Partner together. Although it wasn't my idea, I chose to embrace it. For business owners scraping and scratching to grow, it's hard to imagine sharing contracts with any other company, splitting proceeds that could have been all yours. On paper, my company could have won that contract on a standalone basis. But it made perfect sense on the need to partner. And I would have never done it on my own. Some of my takeaways:

- Be more creative and less greedy. The profits will come when you do the right thing in a joint venture partnership and ensure it's profitable for all parties.
- Bring features of your business with other companies that are similar or complementary and introduce a new way of targeting customers.
- Be willing to use your success to help smaller businesses scale in ways they couldn't on their own.

- Hold your partners accountable and set the standard. Once we began the project, two of my subcontractors weren't following best practices. I had to remove them from our group. But I didn't take their portion of the contract back. I gave it to my other two subcontractors to provide them with more success for being willing to be great subcontractors. A win-win.

We had scaled one of the hardest parts of the mountain and blazed a trail doing it. But I was flaming out. My stamina was giving out. Publicly we had positioned ourselves to reach the pinnacle. Personally, I was disintegrating slowly but surely.

Scaling the Heights

THE 4 PERCENT CLUB (2015–2019)

"It's here!" My receptionist was jumping excitedly and exclaimed as she ran the box back to my office. We recognized the label. The moment had arrived. Everyone gathered around the little box in my office because we were all a part of making this happen. A very big deal indeed. Once opened, there were some streamers and a congratulatory letter nestled inside the box, alongside a complimentary issue of last year's magazine to anticipate how it would look to be in print this year. We didn't know our ranking. That was still a surprise. We only knew that our company made the Inc. 5000 list... for the fifth year in a row!

As indicated by Twintel, "With over 6.1 million companies in the US, only 5,000 of the most innovative and successful companies make the Inc. 5000 list. The Inc. 5000 list is an annual ranking of the fastest-growing private companies in the United States. It ranks the growth of private US companies over a three-year period. It's a highly coveted honor and recognizes your company's achievements (2022).

"But more importantly, being on the Inc. 5000 list shows that you're a serious player in your industry. It's a badge of honor that says you're running a successful business and that you're poised for continued growth. Companies that are on the Inc. 5000 have worked hard to grow and be competitive in their industry. They have also been able to overcome any challenges that come their way and remain successful" (Twintel 2022).

Rankings are based on a three-year sales growth and revenue cycle. As a company's starting revenue base grows after its initial ranking, however, staying on the list in subsequent years becomes more difficult. According to research from Benchworks, "The 2019 Inc. 5000 achieved an astounding three-year average growth of 454 percent, and a median rate of 157 percent. A mere 4 percent of companies have made the list five times" (2019).

How did we grow that much in five years? By making it through four really tough years beforehand and positioning our company for the big leap up.

FIVE STAGES IN FIVE YEARS (2000–2015)

When you start a business from scratch, there is a well-defined path that most take—an evolution of small business growth development for any entrepreneurial startup. This process has been outlined in a classic case from the *Harvard Business Review* (1983), written by Neil C. Churchill and Virginia L. Lewis, which outlines six stages (alongside the challenges presented at each level) for the business owner. I have summarized them as follows:

STAGE I: EXISTENCE
- The owner as the business.
- Challenges are winning customers and sustaining cash for the start-up operation.
- The exit is either to give up and quit if the company a) doesn't gain traction; and/or b) it's too much of a money and time commitment; or c) move on to Stage II (Churchill and Lewis 1983).

STAGE II: SURVIVAL
- The owner may have other employees but still has the primary role.
- The business has won customers, and the focus then shifts to cash flow and profitability.
- The business may stay in this marginal stage and eventually go out of business when the owner gives up or retires or move on to Stage III (Churchill and Lewis 1983).

STAGE III: SUCCESS
- The owner decides whether to keep the company stable and profitable (Churchill and Lewis 1983).

SUBSTAGE III-D
- The owner stays on or hires managers to run the company.
- The business sustains itself unless it is sold, transitions to growth, or becomes susceptible to changing external factors and folds.

- The owner stays active or becomes passive (Churchill and Lewis 1983).

SUBSTAGE III-G
- The owner positions the company for growth, leveraging cash and borrowing power to finance the growth.
- The owner maintains profitability, develops managers, implements systems, and focuses on strategic planning (Churchill and Lewis 1983).

STAGE IV—TAKE-OFF
- Delegation of management to a more complex business structure.
- The owner manages and controls cash with a highly leveraged growth business.
- The owner still has significant presence and control.
- The owner is successful in managing the growth or, if not, they sell the business.
- There are risks if the company grows too fast and runs out of cash, the owner is unable to delegate, or the sales strategy is not achieved.
- The company can either backtrack back to prior stages if unsuccessful or move on to Stage V (Churchill and Lewis 1983).

STAGE V—RESOURCE MATURITY
- Implement further management systems without stifling entrepreneurial qualities.

- Have decentralized organization staff with the owner and the business separate.
- Operate successfully and profitability or move to the quasi-Stage VI (Churchill and Lewis 1983).

STAGE VI—OSSIFICATION
- The company is characterized by a lack of decision-making and risk avoidance.
- Can stay viable unless there is an environmental change that is seized upon by competitors (Churchill and Lewis 1983).

When someone starts a business, it's important to assess the risk and reward and determine what type of success works for that business owner. There are some owners who dip a toe in the entrepreneurial water, and it's not for them. Or it wasn't the right idea or the right timing. But at least they gave it a shot. And perhaps they might take lessons learned from Stage I and try again at some point.

Then there are others who achieve success at either Stage II or Stage III and decide to stay there. It may be a quality-of-life issue. Or there aren't enough resources to drive the company to the next level. These businesses still made it. It's up to the owner to determine how to move out of that stage, if at all. Again, that is also success.

Then there are those entrepreneurs who want to grow and scale. There will be a significant transition in the *company during this stage. The risks get bigger at this stage, yet so do the potential rewards. The owner has to learn to delegate responsibilities while still operating in a fiscally responsible manner. And, of course, **always** watching cash flow (Churchill and Lewis 1983).*

For me, the hardest part of the journey was getting to Stage III. Because it took longer than I thought it would. When we hit Stage IV running in 2015, we had some lost ground to make up. And it was a sprint to the top, as evidenced by the exclusivity of the 4 percent.

THE WINNING COMBINATION
"Kim, would you speak to our sales and marketing group about what you did to grow your business?"

I had joined the local speaker circuit after we achieved much public acclaim within our business community for our high growth. At that time, I was the largest women-owned business in the city of Memphis. It was a great exercise as it crystallized to me what the fundamentals were that drove our topline growth. I reflected back on all the years prior. It definitely wasn't an overnight achievement, and people would probably be shocked to open the cover and understand how difficult those first four years were in getting the business off the ground. It was all part of building our brand and employing specific strategies. What was our specific winning combination? I came up with five key components:

1. CREATE A PRODUCT THAT HAS DIFFERENTIATION IN THE MARKETPLACE.

This piece is critical for any startup entity that wants to exist yet grow. It's what is necessary to drive a business through all the stages. In our first year, we developed the plan and kept refining it through the evolution of the various business cycles.

2. FOCUS ON BRAND IMAGE.

Being the new kid in town with entrenched competition, it was important to get some press in the marketplace. In the very early days, we hired a PR firm to help us place some articles in media outlets. We were able to message our competitive differences in print articles and TV news stories. Then I realized that I could do the same thing with free marketing. I entered every contest available for small businesses. We didn't always win, but even the runners-up got to write about their business. And I used every word the business journals allowed me. We were building our brand at the same time we were building our customer base. The image we consistently messaged was that our company had an innovative approach to delivering security solutions. Oh, and make sure that message is aligned with your marketing. It took me three different iterations of my company website and five years to get that right. It's important.

3. CREATE A WINNING SELLING STRATEGY.

We created what's commonly referred to as a "hunter and farmer" sales model and had the right people in the right positions to supercharge our growth. The hunters gain new business, and the farmers cultivate customer loyalty. In an article from SOCO Sales Management Training, there is a statement I find myself agreeing with: "Building relationships is critical, but sales are what keep the business running. Described as being unwaveringly hungry, eager, not afraid of rejection, and doesn't need convincing to sell more, the Hunter is one of the demanding positions in sales" (2023). And my husband was the best in the business.

4. BECOME SCRAPPY AND FOLLOW WHAT THE MARKET GIVES YOU TO BUILD SPECIALTY NICHES.

When you are building an organic business from the ground up, it's important to consider all opportunities, even if they don't make much sense or don't seem worth the effort. By being scrappy and immediately responsive to fill a need, time and time again, we got our foot in the door with clients, which ultimately led to significantly larger contracts.

5. CONNECT YOUR BUSINESS TO THE LARGER COMMUNITY.

It was this last point that I believe ultimately brought national achievement and recognition to Clarion Security. It's one thing to build a profitable company that supports its employees, returns the investment to the owners, and can create a legacy for future generations. That's a win for employing risk and hard work for your business endeavor. If all you aspire to is to make money, scale, and be acknowledged on the Inc. 5000 list, those are all amazing accomplishments.

I felt that it was another added dimension when you allow yourself to be used in your role as CEO and business owner to impact the larger community around you. To find your passion in something bigger than your company that can impact others both locally and nationally for the greater good. That's a win-win. I knew my community passion, and it aligned with my unique experience. I believed, and I lived it authentically from the start. Small business owners. Minority and women entrepreneurs. And that dedication and giving back, especially to women entrepreneurs, had landed me and my company a prestigious national award.

GROW AT YOUR OWN RISK

There were so many growing pains in that five-year growth explosion journey which I transparently outlined in previous chapters. It's painful to grow that fast. But it is possible. My advice to other entrepreneurs is this: push at your own risk. When you run up that mountain so recklessly fast, it's easy to miss a hazard that can cut you down at a moment's notice.

Did we ever get to Stage V? A few years later, we would find out.

The Pinnacle

October 17, 2017

NAWBO (NATIONAL ASSOCIATION OF WOMEN BUSINESS OWNERS) NATIONAL CONFERENCE
The reality was sinking in fast. I was about to win the national award, and I had no speech. There were three finalists from the nominations across the country. The three women business owners were all there at different tables scattered throughout the large ballroom. You would have thought I had considered writing down some remarks. I mean, "one in three" are decent odds, right? But no. I wasn't doing much thinking ahead those days as I was in the throes of chaos and business execution. The award ceremony had not been at the forefront of my thoughts.

About five minutes before the last and biggest award of the night was presented, it dawned on me that it was a real possibility they were about to call my name. At this point in my business career, I was living off adrenaline, and this was nothing new. I'm also a fantastic procrastinator. I thrive on a deadline, and I have learned to live with the stress and anxiety that was caused by living so far on the edge. I had given impromptu remarks and speeches before. But this may have been pushing it. I had spent zero effort into even roughing out a thank you. This could be a huge failure on the biggest stage I had experienced.

Think it through. Cover the bases, I told myself as I went through in my head what I could come up with on the fly. This was big. There were 1,200 people in the ballroom of the Downtown Marriott Minneapolis, and I was about to be on the big stage giving a speech for a huge national award. It needed to be good.

"And the winner is... Kim Heathcott!"

I was thrilled and excited when I heard my name. I jumped to my feet and immediately headed up to the stage to accept the award, working out my speech with every step. Before I started my company, I had horrible stage fright when I had to give a speech. That was just one of many hurdles I had stepped through running this company. I could give a speech with no issue, but usually that was for about a crowd of twenty to fifty people. Now it was the big leagues.

NAWBO MEMPHIS
Founded in 1975, NAWBO (National Association of Women Business Owners) is a dues-based organization representing the interests of the approximately eleven million women-owned businesses across the country. There are multiple chapters across the country. The first NAWBO Memphis

meeting I attended in 2010 was a small gathering in the back of a Jason's Deli. A bunch of strangers to me that day, I picked up my lunch through the line and sat down and listened as a few speakers talked about their business. There were about ten to fifteen women there, and it was altogether uneventful. I had been embarking on my networking journey across various groups in town. The chamber meeting I attended the week before had about 225 people, a big speaker, and a buzz of energy. This was a meager showing in comparison. From that point on, I latched onto that group and gave them everything I had because of their mission and my desire to further the cause of women entrepreneurs. And I got so much back in return. That day in 2010, I had no idea how impactful that NAWBO Memphis meeting would eventually be for me, personally and professionally.

A national organization with a small local presence. Not really connected with other organizations or influential at the time, but the heartbeat was there, and the local members were earnest and zealous in their dedication to women-owned businesses. I joined the small group. And as with small-fledging groups, there are opportunities to take on responsibilities and leadership—which, as an aside, is often the way opportunities are created. If you have initiative and drive, take those opportunities to bring your creative effort to a worthwhile cause. And those came my way in rapid succession: treasurer, program chair, president-elect, president, board member, and then, finally, volunteering to create a women's business accelerator program for other women business owners as well as running it as cochair for three years. And the more responsibility I took on, the more I dedicated my time and energy to pulling NAWBO and its women members into a seat at the table of Memphis business. Additionally, I also wanted to provide meaningful content for other women entrepreneurs who I felt could benefit from the lessons I had learned in growing my business. I wanted to impart the hard-won wisdom in scaling a business to other women entrepreneurs building their own companies.

Although I took on multiple leadership roles over many years, it was never a solo effort. Together with other women business leaders and officers of the organization, we came together and brought energy, dynamic programs, and a voice to woman-owned businesses. And as we came together and built the chapter, the organization started to grow and take on a new life. And through our collective efforts to grow the chapter and leverage business connections, the chapter got plugged into a bigger entrepreneurial ecosystem at that time in the city that was advocating for growth for women and minority entrepreneurship. We morphed into an organization with an amazing, diverse group of women business leaders with civic and political connections. NAWBO Memphis sisters.

We mattered.

The mayor of Memphis was headed in to say a few words. It was a networking happy hour at the Crescent Club. I was running late, and the event had already started. It was incredible. There must have been over 150 women talking over cocktails. The room was filled with a diverse group. Multi-ethnic, representing the diversity of the city. The mayor stepped to the podium. "I want to congratulate what your organization is doing to promote women- and minority-owned businesses in this city." He gave a quick five-minute speech and headed out the door to his next event. But he wasn't really the main event. It was the relationships and friendships that had grown through the years. Connections and business discussions. Friendships and diversity. It was all there that night. The organization had come a long way from the side room at Jason's Deli five years later.

Looking back, I really didn't have the time that I ultimately put into NAWBO Memphis. But it was like I was compelled by this sense of mission and purpose. I think women leaders, and especially women entrepreneurs, have a bit of a chip on our shoulders in a male-dominated business world. As the largest women-owned business in the city, I felt the responsibility of leading my peers in the best way I could. We were blazing a new trail together, and I was proud to be representing our chapter at the national award ceremony.

But more than that, we had forged a coalition such that my table in Minneapolis at the awards ceremony was filled with my fellow chapter members. When I won the award that evening, I felt I had won it for my friends and peers and for all the women business owners in Memphis.

ENTREPRENEUR AWARDS
"The Woman Business Owner of the Year Award recognizes and rewards a NAWBO entrepreneur who excels at strategy, operations, finances, problem solving, overcoming adversity and giving back to her community. It's not based on business size, but rather overall business excellence" (NAWBO: National Association of Women Business Owners 2023).

For any entrepreneur, winning a national award is a crowning achievement. It validates years of hard work and provides an opportunity to compete at the highest level. There are national lists and awards that offer ways to validate the success of a business.

Inc. 5000 is a national award based solely on revenue growth. Enterprising Women's Enterprising Women of the Year Award is another. Nominees are asked to share three years of revenue history, community/civic leadership, and ways in which they are mentoring or giving back to other women or girls. I was a winner of that award in 2018. So essentially, I was a de facto triple winner in a short period of time. The accolades were compounding in addition to many local and community awards.

I don't think businesses should pursue winning an award as a goal but instead as a by-product of executing a vision and strategy that is impactful on the community. I was and still am passionate and an advocate for women-owned businesses. I dedicated my resources to NAWBO not to win this award someday but instead because I was in the trenches with my business, and I cared about helping others in their endeavors. I spent years putting together this cake. And in this particular moment, for me, it was incredibly sweet icing.

NAWBO AWARD CEREMONY
Earlier that evening on stage, a woman named Jeralynn had come up front and sang an inspirational song that brought the house down. And then, as they gave an introduction that tipped me off to my win, it was my turn. I walked up to the

stage, took a few pictures, turned to the podium, and said to the audience:

"Wow. You know, this is my first year at the NAWBO conference!" I started by poking fun at myself, and everyone laughed right along. My energy had been exclusively committed to my local chapter. I didn't have any relationship with the national organization, which made winning this award so much more humbling. I immediately gave my excuse to justify my absence with NAWBO national. "I've been really working hard these past seven years. I'm blown away by the women in this room." Then I launched into my inspiration. "You know, I have a really strong mother and grandmother. They didn't graduate from college. but they really did the best they could. My mother just retired at seventy-one, and they taught me to work hard." And that was incredibly heartfelt because my mother and grandmother are the most brilliant women I know, but they didn't have the opportunity to leverage the skills in their worlds. "I didn't really think I could be an entrepreneur. But one day, about nine years ago, my husband said, 'You could do it. You can do whatever you want to do.'" Then I let out my heartfelt truth to share with the audience. "Aaagh, I never thought I could run a company." And that was true. I didn't believe in myself and certainly never thought I could accomplish what this business had done in just seven years. "I had a ten-year-old daughter, and I was a stay-at-home mom, and I didn't know a thing. But I knew that I could do this." Now, mind you, I also had a twelve-year-old son when I started, but my point at that moment was to hammer home that I was doing this to be an example for my own daughter. And to honor a legacy from my mother and grandmother, who had the leadership abilities but didn't have the business opportunity that was afforded to me. To show how it was important to be a role model for pushing out of a comfort zone and blazing a trail in whatever endeavor. To show that a woman could do it as well as or better than a man.

And then, it was time to switch gears in the speech. "And the first place I went was to NAWBO Memphis!" That brought a rousing cheer from my table. "And I met some women who helped me out, and I figured 'things' out along the way, and I thought, *You know, it's one day at a time, and I can figure out how to do this.*" That was my shoutout to my sisters and their appreciation back to me for the countless hours I had advocated for all of them. Then, it was time to shift gears to the greater audience. "And throughout the years, I have developed this bond with NAWBO. I'm so proud to be associated with this brand, this national nonprofit that's doing so much for women. Just the energy in what I've learned at this conference is amazing. To represent you and be a part of you wherever you are in business. I want to thank my NAWBO Memphis sisters for nominating me." Then I turned and caught the eye of the side of the stage of the singer, Jeralynn, and I went into improv. "And I want to say that sometimes it's so hard, and if I could have Jeralynn singing to me, maybe it wouldn't be so hard sometimes. I want to record her, and on those hard days, I'm going to keep it going." Even in my improv, it came oozing out the many days of difficulty and hardship. "I want to thank you from the bottom of my heart NAWBO Memphis, NAWBO national, the women who came before me, the women who come after me, and all of you out there who can do incredible things." Then it was time to give my statement of truth. I didn't rehearse it; the words just came out of my mouth because I believed it with every fiber of my being. "I give back to my NAWBO chapter because I believe in women, the power of us, and what we can contribute. And I will do my best to do my part from here on out. So, thank you."

We are better together. That's what I learned from working with NAWBO. The Memphis NAWBO chapter was founded by a visionary and diverse group of women in 1998 who believed in the NAWBO national mission as stated:

As stated on the official NAWBO website, "The National Association of Women Business Owners (NAWBO) propels women entrepreneurs into economic, social and political spheres of power worldwide by:

- "Strengthening the wealth creating capacity of our members and promoting economic development within the entrepreneurial community
- "Creating innovative and effective change in the business culture
- "Building strategic alliances, coalitions and affiliations
- "Transforming public policy and influencing opinion makers" (NAWBO: National Association of Women Business Owners 2023).

As I propelled myself along the journey to get to this pinnacle, I wanted to stand at the top and look across the vista over to the next mountain on the range and see another fellow woman entrepreneur completing her journey to the top. And another. And another. There are not nearly enough of us out there. Plus, if I happened to drop off, I would be grateful that my help and encouragement might have helped someone else get to their pinnacle to continue to lead the cause.

My pinnacle view wouldn't last very long. The air was thinning out, and I was finding it hard to breathe.

PART 5

JOURNEYING DOWN

The Drop

APRIL 13, 2018

The call came in while I was in the small dressing room, trying on dresses that weren't right in the least. It was from the procurement manager from one of the most reputable institutions in the city of Memphis. We were quoting a security bid for them, which was one of the largest private contracts in the city. One that, if we won, could double our size. "Kim, could you explain the bill rates on the quote on page seven? The numbers aren't adding up." Of course I could. I backed out of the dressing room and whispered quickly, "Be right back." My computer went with me wherever I was. I whipped out my laptop in my car and answered the question. Then it was back to the project at hand, which was getting more depressing by the minute.

I looked dejectedly around the store. The black-tie event was in twenty-four hours, and nothing looked right. I was overweight and had waited too long to find an outfit that looked good on me. It had occurred to me a few days prior that I could order a dress online, and I splurged and ordered three of them from Neiman Marcus. Surely one would work. Well, not really, because they didn't arrive until the Monday after the event. This time my procrastination wasn't paying off so well. I only had time to hit a couple of stores to find anything decent. I had spent all my hours working on the giant proposal that was due simultaneously with winning the biggest local award of my career. So far, work was winning, and my priority in self-care and relishing the moment and the ceremony were both losing. That seemed to be my modus operandi of late. It seemed I was putting myself on the back burner once again.

I bought a dress that was subpar. It wasn't really "black tie" quality, though the saleswoman did her best to talk it up. It was a combination paper sack/long bathing suit cover-up in a neutral grayish color. Meant to blend in and cover up—not stand out. Then I went down the retail shopping mall strip and bought some sparkly shoes and a sparkly purse to offset this boring, awful dress and perhaps jazz it up somehow. Done. And then it was back to work on my proposal. I wasn't going to miss that deadline. Friday the thirteenth. Known as a harbinger of bad luck. I hadn't known that it would be the next day, Saturday, April 14, that would be the day that was supposed to be the pinnacle of my career, professionally, but the point of no return for my life personally.

I AM CLARION

It happened all so gradually and seemed so necessary. I needed to build and grow this company for my family's financial future. I placed the responsibility on my shoulders and soldiered up for the journey. But I couldn't carry everything in my backpack as I set off. It was way too heavy and wouldn't last as I set out on the arduous journey. What could I offload?

About a year in, I decided I needed to drop being a leader in my bible study. It was too big of a time commitment. Then it was social activities. I prioritized my children and being present for their activities, and there wasn't enough extra time for friends. Then it was dropping the extracurriculars. No time to play the piano anymore. Or exercise. Or cook. On the weekends, when I could get some work done, it meant no time for church. Or dates with my spouse. Or the energy to talk about anything else but work. I would set up at 7: 00 a.m. at my daughter's swim meet for the next eight hours on a Saturday with my chair right by the outlet so my computer could stay continually charged. I could run into the pool to watch a thirty-second swim, then be back at work for the majority of the day.

As Janna Koretz explains in her article, "What Happens When Your Career Becomes Your Whole Identity," "A particular confluence of high achievement, intense competitiveness, and culture of overwork has caught many in a perfect storm of career enmeshment and burnout" (2019). The storm clouds were swirling all around me and had been for years.

One of the underlying causes she mentions is when career achievements are given a high value by family or community (Koretz 2019). That resonated with me because my entire life had been patterned with a goal of achievement which yielded recognition and acknowledgment. The economic rewards were secondary. It was the "well done" I sought. Whether

I was looking for that from family, peers, or bosses, it was emblazoned in my psyche from an early age.

Then there were other factors. Throwing myself into work helped me avoid feeling emotions that I could bury in my work. This would be called "avoidance coping." As Ciera Graham points out in her blog post "Avoidance Coping: Is It Okay to Escape through Work?" from *Career Contessa*, "For many of us, work has been the only constant aspect of our lives recently—regardless of whatever happens in our world, there will always be work. In a world where we feel like so many events are beyond our control, we can gravitate toward things we feel we *can* control. We bury ourselves in that, which gives us a feeling of accomplishment and gratification—those elements of our lives that are familiar" (2023).

However, it's not a healthy pattern. She goes on to say, "Avoidance coping is a maladaptive form of coping in which a person changes their behavior to avoid thinking about, feeling, or doing difficult things. Avoidance coping is largely unhealthy and counterproductive—it doesn't address the specific stressor, and it does not effectively help us manage stress" (Graham 2023).

What was I avoiding and stuffing down into my backpack? Was I mad that I had to pack that heavy backpack in the first place and carry it on my shoulders? Was I sad that I had to give up things important to me that I valued? I don't know because I just buried all those feelings. I brushed them aside, put the blinders up, and forged ahead. This was the path, and I wasn't going to question it. I was going to get to the top no matter what shape I was in when I arrived.

SOCIETY OF ENTREPRENEURS

Society of Entrepreneurs, a Memphis nonprofit honoring the tradition of entrepreneurship, started in the city from icons such as Kemmons Wilson (Holiday Inn), Pitt Hyde (Autozone), and Fred Smith (FedEx) (SOE Memphis 2023). Each year a small number of new members were voted in on the basis of significant business and civic accomplishments. The award criteria were the following: "Members are chosen annually by their peers, and must be mature (not emerging) entrepreneurs who have exhibited personal business achievement, creativity, determination, integrity, leadership, self-direction and the ability to transform a vision into a dynamic business accomplishment" (2019).

The event was celebrated at a black-tie event with attendees representing prior award winners and current business leaders. I was one of the three inducted on April 14, 2018. It was a tremendous honor. There were only a handful of women who had been inducted prior to me. I had aspired to this award as a dream goal from my first year in business. Back then some of the society members, mature and successful entrepreneurs, had mentored me in those difficult first years. I had listened keenly to their advice and felt like some of the vaunted members had raised me up along the way. It was validating yet so humbling that I was about to be a peer with them in this esteemed society.

There was much pomp and circumstance made of the details leading up to the awards dinner. Part of the process before the awards ceremony was being interviewed for a video that would be shown at the dinner. As is a common thread in my story, I answered off the cuff without prior preparation the day the videographers came to ask me various questions.

My comments tracked a common theme and showed my transparency and honesty. Some of the highlights: "To the chagrin of some of my employees, I like to be in the thick of it all." The negative in that statement was that I acknowledged my micromanagement which, as I had learned, was a symptom of perfectionism. However, the positive was that as a servant leader, I was in the trenches with my employees through good and bad, and I kept pushing our team forward and stayed engaged in every facet of the company. Could we have really accomplished that growth so fast had I not been as engaged? I highly doubted it. But maybe my employees didn't care we were growing as fast as we did. It just meant more problems to manage and overcome. But my intensity didn't relent, and we were all swept up in the momentum together, for better or worse.

In the video, I made my business theory thought statement. "As far as my personal journey in starting a company, you're just not going to know all the answers. You are going to make decisions that are good and bad, and you may learn from it, and that may propel you to the next level. Don't be so hard on yourself. You are going to have failures in addition to success, so make the best decisions you can. Learn from them. And keep moving forward." I certainly had lived that out over and over. If I had said it once, I said it a thousand times: "You don't know what you don't know." Starting, running, and managing a business that scales to the level we did in ten years is a learning curve of gargantuan proportions. And my growth as a leader had also increased in the same proportion.

I just couldn't see it at the time because I was still in a period of burnout and treading water from an emotional standpoint.

But I did take time to write out my speech that year as opposed to the year prior at the NAWBO conference. I gave myself a whole twenty-four hours prior, writing the speech the day before, which was an eternity in my playbook. I considered the message I wanted to convey in just three minutes. My family loves football, and I decided to use a football analogy that had played out in Super Bowl 52 just a few months prior.

Nick Foles of the Philadelphia Eagles began the 2017 NFL season as a backup quarterback, but he finished the year on top of the sports world with a win in the Super Bowl by leading the Philadelphia Eagles to a win over Tom Brady and the New England Patriots. Foles took over the starting role for the Eagles when Carson Wentz suffered a torn ACL. He finished the game with 373 yards, three touchdowns, and one interception, and even caught a touchdown pass. It was the most prolific day of offense in Super Bowl history to date, and the forty-one to thirty-three final score was the second-most points ever scored in the big game. The victory was the first Super Bowl title ever for the Eagles (Stites 2018).

Nick Foles was a largely unknown quarterback, but he rose to the occasion when he had the opportunity to step out on the big stage. And that's how I felt with this opportunity to run this company. My husband had been the MVP of our family for years, starring in one business accomplishment after another. But I was gifted the opportunity to take the leading role this time. I hadn't seen myself as worthy of the starring role in the beginning. Nor did anyone else those many years ago. Yet my husband encouraged me with the belief that I could do this. Like a coach who saw in me a potential raw talent with the skills and abilities to make something tangible and significant. And along the way, I started to believe in myself, not only for myself but as a role model for other women entrepreneurs. The backup quarterback role seemed to be the perfect illustration.

Nick Foles won the Super Bowl 52 MVP that year. And this was my MVP moment. The NAWBO award the year before was a national accomplishment which in itself was hugely significant. And shortly thereafter, I also received an award as CEO of the year from Memphis Magazine. But this ceremony was local acknowledgment among my peers and business associates for the significant accomplishments that I had made as a Memphis entrepreneur of note. And a tremendous honor. After years of agonizing struggle and difficulties, together with tremendous wins and business growth, I received accolades publicly for each role that I had performed with success and public acclaim and acknowledgment.

Woman business owner. Community leader. CEO. Entrepreneur.

The night was incredible. Paper sack dress and all. I felt lifted up by my peers, and the energy in the room was dynamic. My friends and family were all there to cheer me on. I was happy with my video, my fellow women entrepreneur who introduced me did a great job, and I thought my speech was spot on and had a great analogy.

My husband did not. Of the 1,500 people in the room, there was an audience of one who wasn't applauding with the crowd. I didn't understand it at the time. It was lost on me as I took in the moment and only focused on myself and the experience. At the pinnacle of my local business career in the ballroom that evening, in the midst of public accolade, a tipping point had apparently been reached by my spouse. It would then trigger a chain of events that would cause my personal life to spiral down soon thereafter. The role of "wife" was about to come to an end.

I had tried so hard. And it was all for my family, my real team. And how bittersweet that despite my best efforts to perform on the playing field handed to me, negative and intense emotions were churning. Not mine because they were buried deep inside to acquiesce to my will to perform and achieve. Maybe mine were buried so deep that it caused an opposite reaction. Emotions that would erupt and create scenarios that would become catastrophic.

I was about to drop straight off the side of the mountain, and I didn't know how or where I would land.

Kudzu

"I remember family dinners my entire childhood," said my now grown-up daughter to me at lunch. "You and Dad would just talk about the company the whole time, and we just sat there and listened." I sat there in horror as she nonchalantly gave me her version of a family dinner flashback. "We just got used to the fact that you talked about the company nonstop from morning until night."

I wanted to scream back, "We didn't start the company until you were ten years old! Ages two to ten. Those are the golden years of childhood. You don't remember any of those dinners?" But the reality was that none of us really remembered back pre-Clarion. Because the intensity and crisis management that it took to run the company had overtaken our family, like the kudzu vine that grows in the south that smothers out every living plant underneath its path. Normal family routines had been choked out by the trials and tribulations of running our family business.

Not only had my children been pulled into the business as helpers, but they had been front-row spectators to every drama and trauma played out at night, on the weekends, on family trips and holidays. And clearly, from my daughter's recollection, every night at dinner. We allowed our personal life to be choked out because we didn't put adequate or sufficient boundaries in place to stop the disastrous spread of company business into our family.

Then there was the impact on my marriage. According to the article "5 Tips for Running a Business with Your Spouse" from CEO Today, "Having your own business is already a challenge, but sharing it with a spouse could be a disaster" (2021). Well, too bad I couldn't go back in time and read the five tips for not running the ship up on the rocks. As I reviewed the five, it was a personal road map from well-intentioned to shipwreck.

"Have Well Defined Roles and Responsibilities. Division of labor will create order and structure for your business. Also, it will ensure you will not step on each other's toes. Assign and designate tasks by playing up to your strengths" (CEO Today 2021).

Grade A++ in this arena. I would argue there were not two people with more complementary skills starting a business. I believe that's what kept our company on the right trajectory for success. And it's a lesson regardless of whether you run a family business or not. Play to your strengths and surround yourself with the ones that you lack. This one was what we got right, but it also didn't involve emotional issues. It was when we added those stressors that things started to falter.

"***Separate Work from Personal Life.*** *To ensure a healthy work-life balance, set clear business hours and respect them. Set weekly or monthly meetings where you discuss the most important issues related to your business. In the dedicated time-span, you can also brainstorm solutions for existing problems and give each other feedback. Also, make sure you choose your time carefully not to ruin quality time with your family. When having dinner or playing with the children, commit fully to those activities*" (CEO Today 2021).

So, clearly, a Grade F on that one. A failure across the board. A lack of boundaries, which bled over into family time constantly right from the beginning. The marriage became the company and our children the collateral damage in the storyline.

"***Set Clear Boundaries.*** *Working together should not rob you of your individuality. Try setting up different work-spaces, which you can arrange to your liking. Spending some work-time separately can be beneficial for both your business and marital relationship*" (CEO Today 2021).

Grade B. It was too much of a good thing. Working together. Lunching together many days. Offices right across the hall from one another.

"***Focus on Communication.*** *Communication is essential in all areas of life. Therefore, make sure you talk over everything before making a final decision. Do not hesitate to bring up any concerns you may have. When discussing an issue, never blame the person; instead, address the action that led to a problem*" (CEO Today 2021).

Business—grade B. Personal, grade F. We were really great at this on business topics. The ying offsetting the yang. I only give this a B because the communication was on a nonstop basis that had no boundaries. If an issue needed processing while brushing teeth in the morning, then it was. Not healthy but realistic. However, from a personal standpoint, the communication ground to a halt. The personal connection prior to this company was overrun by the issues and problems of the company. There was no room left to talk about life outside of the company.

"*Offer Each Other Constant Support. You and your partner are in this together. It is important to know that you can rely on each other. Therefore, always be there for one another, be ready to offer help and emotional support. Another way you can show support is by refraining from micromanaging. This will only show that you do not trust your partner to do their tasks. If for any reason your joint business venture did not work out, it might be time to contact legal experts. Qualified family law attorneys can help protect your shared business even if you decide to break a partnership in marriage*" (CEO Today 2021).

Wow. I couldn't believe the author of this article just put that cold statement out there. But the truth is that somewhere along the way, the support was lost. Maybe in the emotional stress of the day-to-day operation. Or the imbalance of perceived power. Or the emphasis on being a women-owned business prioritized over a partnership and family business.

What could I have done differently?

I've asked myself that question a million times over. Where could I have implemented those boundaries that could have potentially stopped the damage before it could take hold and cause permanent harm to a marriage? In the very beginning, I could have said, "No, thank you, but I will not start a security guard company." Because it originally was not my dream and at first I did not want it to be my reality. But I wasn't nearly that strong. Plus, I'm a fixer. Give me a problem, and I want to solve it, no matter whether it's really my problem to solve or not. Then add that I'm a recovering people pleaser. I want to make everyone happy while I fix the problem that wasn't mine in the first place and make sure everyone is okay. Never mind me. Then there's the last one: I really want to hear the "well done."

The key issues here are that I accepted too much responsibility to remedy a situation that involved two people. And then the company became missional to me as a women-owned business. Whether that was wrong or right, it was the reality. I'm also a very black-and-white thinker. I would own it and make it work. And it did, and the company became amazingly successful, albeit at a severe cost to my personal life. Was there an alternative to the initial design of the company? Were we successful because the company was a woman-owned business and I was compelled to make it all the way to the top? Or could we have been equally successful as a true 50/50 partnership that could have preserved our family by not shifting the balance of power? Unfortunately, it would be a question never answered.

Kudzu is almost impossible to eradicate once established. It's a beautiful lush green leaf that covers trees, ground, and even inanimate objects. It's a canopy of leaves that blankets a landscape from one end to another. From a distance, it's a beautiful sight. But, up close, it's a smothering of something beautiful that existed in a unique form underneath it that is dying from the inside out.

And after ten years of running the company, that's where we ended up. This business venture that we entered into for our family legacy was what ultimately smothered our family unit. Although we committed both our skills and talents to make the business tremendously successful from a financial standpoint, the costs had multiplied on the personal front and had not been caught in time to remedy.

Clarion cares. But at what cost to a marriage, a family, a dream, our future? It was slipping away, and I didn't have the capacity at the time to unwind the spiraling down process that had taken hold. There were too many unhealthy patterns to unwind. Too much erosion of trust. Too much abdicating of personal relationships to focus on a business. All we could do at that point was try to quell the damage and figure out how on earth to unwind a life, a marriage, a family, and a business that were all intertwined in that poisonous kudzu blanket.

I had a lot of decisions to make.

Decisions

"When do you want to set the wedding date?" It was a tough decision. I was halfway through the SMU twenty-month executive MBA program. We graduated in May 1996. I was living and working in Dallas and planning a wedding in Memphis, which in itself was a stressor. *Do I wait until after graduation?* That was one choice. Then there was my stubborn self that kicked in. *Why should my personal life be put on hold?* Hence the decision was made. "Let's plan the wedding for April 1996!" I guess I had it all worked out in my head. I'll plan a wedding in another city, transition my career, plan a wedding long distance, and then get married, all the while meeting the demands of my job and graduate school. *What could go wrong?*

According to a blog post from HubSpot, written by Leslie Ye, "Choice is the purest expression of free will—the freedom to choose allows us to shape our lives exactly how we wish (provided we have the resources to do so). Choice theory is the study of how decisions get made. The term was coined in a book of the same name by William Glasser, who argued that all choices are made to satisfy five basic needs: survival, love and belonging, power, freedom, and fun" (2019).

She continues, "Choice is difficult because it also represents sacrifice. Choosing something inherently means giving up something else—something we might want tomorrow, or next week—and that won't be available to us if we don't grab it today" (Ye 2019).

At thirty-two years old, when faced with an intersection of major personal and professional commitments, I didn't want to sacrifice anything in either arena. I chose to start a serious long-distance relationship while retaining a full-time job and committing to an intense graduate school program. That just doesn't work on paper. My stubbornness and lack of conscience regarding my mental health and self-care all worked together to conspire to my brain that I really could do it all and have it all at once. In reality, there weren't enough hours in the day to give all three my best. And that became my pattern for life: overcommit, take on too much responsibility, and don't set boundaries to take care of yourself. And plow ahead. Juggle all the balls in the air and hope you don't drop them all at the same time. Or hope you don't crash to the ground with the balls hitting the ground right behind you.

Now here I was again in the same situation. Twenty years later, I repeated the same thing. How did I get back to that unhealthy dynamic? I had chosen differently for an interlude. I had given up my professional life to focus on my family and raise my children. I had become content with a life that was in balance. I had chosen my priorities, and I was healthy and happy. Then this life-changing career choice was presented to me. It really felt at the time as if the choice was pushed on me. I could have said no. But I'm not sure I knew how to do that at the time. Thus, I entered entrepreneurship feeling both reluctant and resistant. I was apprehensive as I took back a double stack of family and a demanding career.

In running the company, I went back to the default mode that I had learned years prior. Push myself to the limit in time, energy, and dedication to causes important to me and my family, with little to no regard for the impact on my personal well-being. At thirty years old, I could somewhat handle it. At fifty-five years old, it was too much. With my mental and physical well-being shot, my marriage tanking, and my company grinding me up, I realized the sacrifice I was making was of my choosing. And crashing to the ground with my juggling balls surrounding me, I didn't have the energy to pick them up anymore.

All choices have consequences, sooner or later. Some you'll feel more than others. In general, though, the more mindful you are of the potential consequences, the more likely you will make better choices. That would be a lesson learned the hard way. Clearly, I hadn't caught on the first time. It was rinse-and-repeat for a time—until the consequences forced me to take action and make really hard choices.

It was time to choose survival. Love, power, freedom, and fun were going to have to take a back seat. And the choice was not for my family, our financial future, my marriage, or our children. It was finally time to choose survival for me. If I was going to peel myself up off the cold pavement, I was going to have to make some hard decisions that put myself at the center of my priority list for the first time in a long time.

LEAVING CLARION

It hadn't been easy. As a matter of fact, it had been one of the most agonizing decisions of my life. Was I really going to relinquish my company? There was so much tied up in that decision. The company had become like a third child. It had taken on a significance in my life that would be incredibly difficult to walk away from. Then there were my employees. I felt like I was the best person to take care of them. That if I left the company to someone else's leadership, then they might not be cared for in the same manner as I would.

Would a different leader care for my people as I cared for them? Would bottom-line results be the priority and cause some of my policies to be eliminated? Would the company revert to the typical leadership model of my competitors?

I had a lot of fear in those moments. Would my legacy be slowly erased as the company moved past me? There are six different prominent leadership styles. One is not better than the other. They are just different. I led completely aligned with my values and my core. It worked for those ten years. All I could do was be grateful for the past and stop worrying about the future of the company. I made a difference, and eventually, my chapter came to an end. I could walk away and leave the rest of the story in others' leadership styles.

Then there was the financial decision to walk away from a successful and profitable company. Those many lean years had turned into years that were bountiful. Yet as I considered the monetary ramifications, I realized there were other intangibles pulling me away that were more significant than just a financial play. The security guard industry, and even this company, hadn't been my idea. I had made it my own over the years, but the opportunity was manufactured from other agendas than mine from the beginning. Now that I knew how to run a company, there were businesses I could run or start that were much more suited to my personality. That wouldn't cause me such a strain by pulling against my natural personality 24/7. And in the end, I determined that money was not the top consideration.

Then there was the ego factor. Was my identity wrapped up in being a CEO and a business owner? Would I retain the company because that was top of mind and critically important? Ultimately, it wasn't. My whole bent as a business owner was as a servant leader. This experience was so much more than checking a box and feeling self-important being on top of a pyramid. I had left a career once before and never looked back. I could leave this one now. After the emotion wore off, I would be okay. However, I chose to land career-wise, even if it meant starting completely over.

But then there was the larger community to consider. Would I let down my fellow women business owners if I walked away from Clarion Security? That was much more piercing to my psyche. I didn't want to abandon the company and send a message that this was all for nothing. That the largest women-owned company in Memphis, Tennessee, was no more, and I was leaving my sphere of influence, which also included entrepreneurs and other women business owners who were also friends and peers.

This one was hard. I could only hope if I walked away that they would support my decision and consider other factors were at play and appreciate what I gave back for the time I was in that role.

Those were some of the external stressors weighing on my decision. How would I decide?

First, I considered the options.

- Could I run a company with a business partner being a former spouse? That seemed fraught with boundary issues. And I knew I struggled in that arena.
- Should I sell the company to a third party? It would have resolved things nicely, and everyone could close the chapter and move on. But, the buyer would probably be a large behemoth company who could strip our management team dry. And how would they treat our customers? I had concerns about that option.
- Sell the company to my husband. Preserve a potential legacy company for our children. Hand the keys over and let the company evolve into the next phase under his sole leadership. Relinquish control and move on.

I wrestled for months over the best course of action. There are pros and cons to each choice. For any entrepreneur, it is tremendously difficult considering how to move back or away from a company so passionately built with your footprint all over it.

If business owners are considering a decision to shift ownership, leave, or sell a business, I would recommend engaging trusted advisors and confidants who know the situation and can best advise you as to the best option. I had tremendous advice which helped me navigate an emotionally charged situation. Peers, friends, and family who could see the bigger picture and help move me to the best choice.

Ultimately, it came down to what would bring peace and the best resolution for all family members. And that was to sell to my husband and move on. After ten incredibly tumultuous years, that decision was the best one on the table for many reasons. It allowed me to take a respite and focus on my self-care. To reinvent myself once more with the lessons learned. To give myself some grace. And also to be grateful I had an impact on hundreds of people that hopefully had a positive ripple effect from the compassionate moves I had made in my business model. It was okay to leave.

I was taking a giant step in setting a boundary and saying no to the company and saying yes to what I needed in the moment and, ultimately, for my future. As Sadie Hinkel points out in the article "The Importance of Boundaries and Saying No," "Even though no is just a two-letter word, it can carry quite a bit of guilt and pressure" (2022). I saw myself in her caution. She continues, "Giving too much of yourself to others can result in bitterness or resentment, which is harmful to any relationship, whether it's a professional or personal relationship" (Hinkel 2022).

In the scheme of boundaries, after a tortuous decision process, this would be a giant *no* with many ramifications. Once

I made the decision, there was a follow-up question. Was Clarion ready to move on without me?

It was time to test whether we had moved to Stage V as defined in the "Five Stages of Small Business Growth" (Churchill and Lewis 1983).

STAGE V—RESOURCE MATURITY

"A company in Stage V has the staff and financial resources to engage in detailed operational and strategic planning. The management is decentralized, adequately staffed, and experienced. And systems are extensive and well-developed. The owner and the business are quite separate, both financially and operationally (Churchill and Lewis 1983).

"The company has now arrived. It has the advantages of size, financial resources, and managerial talent. If it can preserve its entrepreneurial spirit, it will be a formidable force in the market" (Churchill and Lewis 1983).

Thankfully the work had been done to reach this stage, and I could hand it off without issue. I had delivered my part in the stage transition. The company was ready to run without me at the helm. We had moved through to the final stage. Clarion was ready for the next leader and the next phase. My work there was done.

It didn't have to be a drop or fall down the mountain. Rather than tumble uncontrollably to the bottom, I was able to catch myself and walk deliberately and steadily down the mountain step by step. I had seen the pinnacle view and analyzed it from a 360-degree perspective. I had learned from the journey and conquered amazing milestones. It was now time to come down from the mountain in a sure-footed way and take a well-deserved respite.

PART 6

SURVEYING THE VISTA

Reinvention

"Is it ok if I come over now?" Renette called to ask.

"Sure," I responded flatly.

I had nothing but time. My world was silent and still and somewhat stifling. Timing is everything. I sold the company on March 5, 2020, one week prior to the entire world being flipped upside down from the pandemic. It had been over a month, and I was living in this space of suspended time where nothing made sense. I had unraveled the last vestiges of connections to the business and was no longer needed there. But I had nothing to propel me forward because of the pandemic shutdown. I felt both paralyzed and marginalized. I was still processing the grief that comes with significant loss, coupled with the chaos of the present and uncertainty of the future.

The doorbell rang. I opened the door, and Renette entered, bringing balloons, a card from the office staff, and a personal gift—the last tangible remnants of my going away party that got canceled with the COVID-19 shutdown. It was now just a party of two. It was a fitting end to my involvement with Clarion Security. My business was significant in the ways It had benefitted the people involved with it. And my heart was grateful that, despite the sacrifices and tolls taken on our personal lives, Renette and I had worked together to create a company with purpose. A mission that meant something to both of us that had taken on a greater significance and meaning in its execution. A company that would ultimately continue on without me, strong and positioned for further success.

As she handed me the last few of my things in a container, I realized I had just been handed my own to-go box from Clarion, like one of the holiday meal containers I used to hand out. Conveying a token of appreciation for dedication to the work performed, I was now on the other side as a recipient. The last vestige of what was mine, now packaged up in a disposable container and given to me as I stood there, alone, watching the car with the Clarion logo fade off in the distance.

I could look at the gift one of two ways. I could discount it as a meaningless token and symbolically throw it in the trash. Or I could consider it a representation of the care it took to provide me a way to be able to go. In the moment, I was too wrapped up in grief to consider anything positive. Yet perhaps the ability to go was the greatest gift I could have been given.

And that was the end of my chapter. My final sendoff pared down to a few token items. It was anti-climactic and somehow devoid of emotion. I had been wrung dry getting to that point. There were no more tears left, no more sleepless nights, and no more negotiations. One final goodbye. At least it was from someone who truly did care.

So far, I was batting zero in 2020. But I was tired of sitting around in the inertia of sadness and depression. And circumstances were bumping up right to my backyard, propelling me into action. I had dealt with obstacles before and never let them stop me. Enough was enough. The pandemic was a worthy foe, but I needed to push through and start moving forward. It wouldn't take me long to take the next step.

A NEW BEGINNING
A bright, beautiful morning with the sun behind me glistening off the silver arching bridge spans. As I hit the Mississippi River bridge headed west on the I-40 that May morning, it felt like I was leaving everything I had. And I was, really. Everything except the two family cats I retained in the divorce, crying in the passenger seat in furious protest of being caged up and pulled out of their peaceful home base.

But as loudly as they were protesting, I was matching them in silent shock. I had spent the last two weeks in a moving frenzy. Cataloging possessions, sorting them into keep or store, leasing an apartment over the internet, renting my house in a day because I put my house on the market the week of the country's shutdown and no one wanted to buy a house in the early pandemic scare. I had made the decision to pick up and run in two weeks' time. An aggressive timetable after shutting down a twenty-four-year marriage, leaving a ten-year business with the entire world shut down around me. The inertia had paralyzed me for a short time, but I reenergized once the decision was made.

I hit the bridge with little to no traffic. No one was on the roads anymore since the country was shut down and barely anyone was driving. I had a clear and easy path to Dallas. As I drove onto the massive bridge arching over the vast Mississippi River, the open and empty road ahead flashed into my psyche and registered to my mind that my current life and future were both open and empty. At fifty-five years old, I was leaving behind my family and friends, my church, my marriage, my business network, and my company. All those identities eradicated every mile I marked headed west.

CEO, woman business owner, wife. Gone and finished. That chapter of my life had closed. And it was so hard shutting down those identities that I decided I needed a clean break and a new city, even though that would cause me to give up my entire support system as well. I needed a new place to start over because giving up the company as well as the marriage had taken two agonizing years. And I just couldn't play those tapes anymore in my head in the world that had existed for both. Tennessee to Texas in two weeks with two cats.

At that moment, I didn't know what was in store for the rest of my life. I only knew that once I hit the bridge, that twenty-four-year chapter was really over. It was real, and I had made it happen. And, in that moment, I felt good. Buoyed that I was making a decision forward even though I had no idea what it would look like on the other side. All I knew was that the unknown in Texas outweighed the pain in Tennessee.

It was time to choose me.

So I crossed that bridge and left my life behind in hopes I would renew and start fresh in a new way. I was by myself now. It was time to figure out what I really wanted out of my life in my next chapter. What my true identities were, and how I would move forward in the best version of Kim. New Kim.

STARTING OVER

Where would I begin? As eloquently stated by Ali Hall, "Life is full of new beginnings, whether you want it or not. And with a bit of preparation, these new starts don't have to be so scary. The grief of an ending can distract us from focusing on the exciting birth of a new beginning" (2023). I was ready to shake off that grief with every mile that ticked off to my do-over.

Hall offers these five ways to help someone start over:

1. "Reconnect with yourself and make changes necessary to live authentically aligned with your values.
2. "Learn new skills.
3. "Be open to new people and experiences.
4. "Shake away bad habits.
5. "Embrace the fear" (2023).

Fear. There it was again. In the past, fear had paralyzed me, causing me to give in to anxiety and avoidance. Now it was time to push through fear, embrace the change, and see the possibilities on the other side. I had gotten this far. I was on the road. It was time to see what could be waiting for me at the new destination. But in order to see it, I had to shift my focus and begin to discover myself again.

So I stopped looking back in the mirror, the cats got tired of crying, and we all finished the journey, quietly focused ahead. By that evening, I was sitting on the balcony of my twenty-fifth floor apartment overlooking the Dallas downtown skyline. Shiny, sparkling lights, glowing and flickering from building to building, created a colorful panorama that radiated energy and mesmerized me. And as my view panned from east to west, I realized this was a brand-new mountain range to explore. So many possibilities. Whenever I was ready.

Refreshment

"Is that the book you keep reading by those 'happy people'?" she asked in a sardonic tone. But I knew behind the tone was love and empathy for me and my efforts to change my outlook and perspective. We were sitting on the beach with feet in the sugar white sand and lounge chairs facing the turquoise waters off the Gulf Coast of the Florida panhandle. Highway 30-A, a twenty-mile scenic highway route between Destin and Panama City filled with quaint beach towns and amazing beaches. My happy place with my best friend. I was on a journey to find happy and was discovering it in multiple ways.

It was about time.

THE SCIENCE OF WELL-BEING (HAPPINESS)

It turns out I wasn't the only one looking for happiness. When Laurie Santos, Yale professor, put her wildly popular college class on the internet in 2020, millions of people signed up for the free class. As detailed on Coursera, "Professor Laurie Santos reveals misconceptions about happiness, annoying features of the mind that lead us to think the way we do, and the research that can help us change" (Coursera 2023). The course offers quantifiable research on what elevates a person's well-being or happiness (spoiler alert—money doesn't buy happiness) (Elassar 2022). It was one of the first things I did for myself once I got to Dallas.

So what are the five practices to elevate happiness, based on scientific research? Laurie Santos outlines these tips:

GET SOCIAL
"When psychologists Ed Diener and Marty Seligman looked at people who scored in the highest tenth percentile on happiness surveys, they discovered that there was one activity that set happy people apart from the rest of us—happy people were more social. The results were so strong that these researchers deemed being around other people as a necessary condition for very high happiness" (Santos 2020).

GIVE THANKS
"Another way to supercharge well-being is with a dose of gratitude—the simple act of stopping to consider all the good things in your life. Research shows that grateful people—those who count their blessings on a regular basis—experience a host of benefits. Grateful people tend to be happier and show lower levels of stress hormones like cortisol" (Santos 2020).

BE IN THE MOMENT

"One study by a team of Harvard psychologists found that we spend more than 40 percent of the time mind-wandering—not paying attention to the here and now. Which is bad news for our happiness levels, because a growing body of research shows that focusing on the here and now makes us feel better" (Santos 2020).

REST AND MOVE

Examples she offers are meditation to help put negative thoughts in perspective so they depart instead of causing us to act on them. And paying attention to details in our current world that are positive and good that we enjoy and bring pleasure, and also getting a good night's sleep and exercise (Santos 2020). "One study found that doing a half-hour of cardio on a stationary bike reduces the likelihood that we'll feel things like tension, anger, depression, and even fatigue. And the effect was shown to last for over twelve hours" (Santos 2020).

BE KIND

"Research shows that we get happiness from doing nice things for other people. The people who self-report being happiest are focused on those in need—they donate more of their time and money to charity and engage in random acts of kindness" (Santos 2020).

Santos also reminds us to be kind to ourselves. "Research shows that our inner brutal drill sergeant isn't as motivating as we assume. Harsh self-criticism and unrealistic expectations will destroy your morale and make you give up before you even begin. A better strategy is to extend yourself some kindness, or what psychologists call self-compassion. Self-compassion means remembering that you're human and that—just like everyone else on the planet—you're doing the best you can in some pretty tough times" (Santos 2020).

My takeaway from the course and the research is that each one of us can shift our attitudes and perspectives to achieve a happier life. It's not dependent on other people or things. And we can start over daily by putting in some simple practices to shift our mindset. But equally as important is being intentional about connecting with other people and taking the time and effort to engage with others. Life was never intended to live alone. I may not have been married anymore, but I was never alone. Those relationships that had fallen by the wayside while I was running the company were there, just lying dormant. It's amazing how when you choose to invest in other people's lives and cultivate those relationships again, they spring back to life.

Taking that course was what I needed to stay in the moment and not be tempted to look back with eyes of regret considering the what-ifs, but instead to just accept and appreciate the opportunity to learn and grow in the moment. If you stumble and get lost on a mountain, would you retrace your steps all the way to the bottom and start over? Probably not. You would consult the map and the compass and get back on track, tools to help guide your way.

I needed additional strategies and tips to "get back to happy." Thus, I found the happy people, Marc and Angel Chernoff.

As described on their Marc and Angel Hack Life page, "Marc and Angel Chernoff are *New York Times* bestselling authors, professional coaches, full-time students of life, admirers of the human spirit, and have been recognized by *Forbes* as having 'one of the most popular personal development blogs.' Through their blog, books, courses, events, and coaching, they've spent the past fifteen years writing about and teaching proven strategies for finding lasting happiness, success, love, and peace" (2023).

In a blog post titled "10 Wake-Up Calls People Receive Too Late in Life," one of Angel Chernoff's points resonated with me: "Behind every beautiful life, there has been some kind of worthwhile pain" (2023).

She continues, "You trip and you fall, you make mistakes and you fail, but you stand strong through it all—you live and you learn. You're human, not perfect. You have been wounded, not defeated. Think of what a priceless gift it is to grow through these experiences—to breathe, to think, to struggle, and to overcome challenges in the pursuit of the things you love. Yes, sometimes you will encounter heartache along the way, but that's a small price to pay for immeasurable moments of love and joy. Which is why you must keep stepping forward even when it hurts, because you know the inner strength that has carried you this far can carry you the rest of the way" (2023).

It was time to move forward. Step. To grow and change. Step. To make the choice for happiness. Step. To appreciate the past, hope for the future, yet live and relish the present... Step.

And as I focused on getting healthy and happy personally, I was taking small steps forward in my journey to recast my career. I wasn't ready to scale another mountain. They were all around me, but I needed some time and space to make sure I was going to pick the one that was best for me to climb if and when I was ready. Because next time, I wanted to appreciate the journey all the way up. When I reached that next pinnacle, I didn't want it to be from grit and grind but from a place of strength and wisdom.

For now, I was perched on a ledge, looking across to the mountains with renewed peace and strength and being content with exactly where I was. Bathed in the sunlight of refreshed vision and contentment and appreciation of just staying right there in the moment.

Reflections

It's quiet again. The days of chaos and drama seem way in the rear-view mirror. It feels amazing to come back to center and connect soul and body and mind together in a positive, healthy way. To be able to look at past history with eyes of grace and compassion for all the players, including myself.

It's not easy to start over. To release identities that brought confidence, self-esteem, and value. My bittersweet ending to an amazing chapter as a business owner. The company still runs well, just without me at the helm. My children move forward in life without me as a caregiver now that they are adults. My role as wife ended after twenty-four years. A community of women business owners continue to make strides forward without me as a leader and champion.

But starting over doesn't mean giving up. I got stuck there for a moment. "Why did it all happen this way?" I say to myself with sadness and disappointment in melancholy moments when I look back to the past. Then I fight my way out of that thought with belligerence jumping straight to a fighting future. "I'll prove my worth and solidify my business record by creating a company bigger and better in my next journey!" But that's just vacillating between feeling sorry for myself and letting my ego drive my thoughts instead of what is important—appreciating the now and present.

REFLECTIONS ON ENTREPRENEURSHIP

What lessons can I take away from my entrepreneurial journey to the top? We had unusually extraordinary success in ten years. Were we an anomaly?

According to data from the Bureau of Labor Statistics, as reported by Fundera, "Approximately 20 percent of small businesses fail within the first year. By the end of the second year, 30 percent of businesses will have failed. By the end of the fifth year, about half will have failed. And by the end of the decade, only 30 percent of businesses will remain—a 70 percent failure rate" (2020).

Those are sobering statistics. And I believed them because, in those first five years, we teetered on the brink of failure many times over. Lack of revenue, running out of cash, unexpected expenses, and operational setbacks. We had them all and then some. So why was my business one of the 30 percent that survived past the ten-year mark?

People often think of entrepreneurs as individuals who come up with a brilliant idea and build a company around an invention, such as Steve Jobs or Elon Musk. Then there are those who come up with an innovative idea and execute it well, such as Fred Smith, Sam Walton, and Jeff Bezos. The perception is that there has to be an original idea behind the company. I would argue that there are just as many successful entrepreneurs that take a common industry and put their spin on delivery and culture. Southwest Airlines and REI as examples.

Then there are those countless companies that look at a mature product or service and differentiate their company that also have tremendous success in normal, everyday businesses. And I think that's where most entrepreneurs land. Especially ones without extensive access to capital, an innovative invention, or the knowledge base to manufacture a product. Often, it's the companies that are started up when someone has some basic knowledge of the industry and the ones that require the least minimal investment in startup costs. That's how my company was started.

But even if you have a good or great idea, I believe it is most often the personality of the business owner that drives the startup venture. There are those intangible traits of the leader that cause a company to be either a success or a failure. I believe it takes a combination of character traits with some basic skills that can create a lasting entrepreneurial venture that can make it through the startup phase. And these are a must:

- Determination
- Stamina
- Passion
- Drive
- Resourcefulness
- Hard worker
- Self-disciplined

Starting up a company is not for the faint of heart. A competitive mindset that believes you can succeed, with the hard work backing you up, are required components. In those first five years, I believe it was these foundational traits I possessed that kept my company from failing.

But what if you have all those character traits and your business doesn't make it? According to Michael Deane, as stated in an article for *Investopedia*, here are the top six reasons:

1. "Not investigating the market
2. "Business plan problems
3. "Too little financing
4. "Bad location, internet presence, and marketing
5. "Remaining rigid
6. "Expanding too fast" (2022)

In other words, it is necessary to have a product or service with a market differentiator to the existing competitive landscape, a methodical approach, adequate financing sources, a sound marketing plan, and an ability to learn from mistakes and manage growth. Nowhere in that list is a brilliant and novel idea that has never been done. Sometimes the best entrepreneurial ventures take existing ideas in the market and make them better. A solid business venture combined with a business owner who has the ability to bring it to fruition. And that is exactly what we had and how I executed our plan successfully.

Almost half of start-ups in 2021 were formed by women, according to human resources cloud software company, Gusto (Masterson 2022). That's an impressive number. Then layer on the research from *Harvard Business Review*, which indicates that more than two-thirds of new businesses, in general, never realize a return and fail to return any investment (Eisenmann 2021).

So why do startups gain traction yet fail to ever return an investment? Perspective for the top six reasons is given by David Skok, a serial entrepreneur. The major reasons for the failure of return on investment, regardless if its owner is a woman or man, are as follows:

1. Market problems—not a compelling enough value proposition or wrong market timing.
2. Failure to develop a product that meets market need due to execution and/or strategy.
3. Failure to find a *repeatable* and *scalable* sales growth model.
4. Failure to find a *profitable* growth model.
5. Poor management team.
6. Running out of cash (Skok 2010).

I believe this list also relates to small businesses that have achieved initial success just with the business owner(s) but don't have a framework for growing and scaling the business. Hiring employees, securing financing, and implementing systems and processes. How do they take those next steps? I would concur these components are critical on their journey should they embark on it.

REFLECTIONS ON MY JOURNEY

An entrepreneur who pushes to the limits mentally and physically may well eliminate one of the character traits of any successful entrepreneur: *stamina*. According to Merriam-Webster, the definition of stamina is the bodily or mental capacity to sustain a prolonged stressful effort or activity.

And that's why I ultimately walked away from my company. After ten years, I left everything I had on the field, and I was no longer capable of continuing in my role. The burnout was real, and I couldn't roll it back. It wasn't a failure to walk away. It was an acknowledgment that, at that moment, I was incapable of any more; that I would call the ten years a success and step away in order to build back the stamina for another venture if and when it was the right time.

With the opportunity to build Clarion Security to national acclaim, I was pushed out of my comfort zone and made to embrace my natural abilities and make a mark for myself, my family, my community, and for women entrepreneurs. I may not be running that company, but I'm changed forever from that experience. And can't I leverage that experience in a way that can impact others to blaze their own trail?

I will always be an entrepreneur. But it can look completely different from my past track record and still be called successful. I just needed a minute to catch my breath. I still have a spark, a chance, a voice, a path. There may be another mountain for me to climb and see if I can make it to the top. Or maybe I'm meant to help others climb their own mountains. For now, I'm just taking one step at a time. The key is to move. And if it takes a bit of time, that is all right with me. I've already come down from the mountain and landed on my feet. I'm moving along the next journey to success at a much slower pace to preserve the stamina I worked hard to build back.

And what about you? Don't let the setbacks and some of my personal failures deter you from starting or continuing your own journey up, up, up. If you ask me, I would say it was worth every minute of the journey. Remember when I hit the top of the mountain, battle-scarred and weary, covered with dirt and grime? When I looked down and realized what I had accomplished, my view was marked with much joy.

I hope my stories, advice, failures, and personal challenges have put down some markers to help you get to your respective pinnacle or will help you come down the mountain if you need your own respite and opportunity for refreshment in order to try again.

Where do you want to start climbing? Or do you need to get back on your feet in order to start moving again?

It's never too late.

Acknowledgments

I would like to thank my mom, who read my first manuscript and still encouraged me to keep going. The first version was clearly for just you and me. I'm so thankful I have this version to share with everyone else. You are *my* role model.

To my Sea Island Seven peers and amazing women entrepreneurs, thank you for your encouragement and support in helping me down the mountain and keeping me focused on what the future could hold.

To my "Vandy Girls" friends, your feedback that I was a good storyteller motivated me so many times in this book writing journey. Now that I've written down some of them, I hope to be one of your book club selections one day! And Tammy, thank you for being my beta reader on a tight deadline!

To my daughter Laura Lane, I would have given up long ago if you hadn't been my biggest cheerleader. I am beyond grateful for your inspiring support and belief in me. How can I ever let you down?

To my son Jack, your words back to me on the impact of leading this company on your life are all I ever really needed.

To April, there are no words. Just my heartfelt love and appreciation for you. I know that you know.

To my NAWBO Memphis sisters, I miss you and appreciate all your support through the years.

To Larry, thank you for believing in me and all the work you did as we achieved much together. I wish you continued great success leading the charge on your own journey.

To Denise, thank you for your "rockstar" encouragement on this book-writing journey.

To my amazing development editor, Angela Ivey, and amazing revisions editor, Heather Romanowski, your even-handed feedback and support gave me the blueprint to keep pushing forward. I am forever grateful for your diplomacy and keen insights, which allowed me to take things deeper and fuller.

I'd also like to thank Eric Koester and the incredible team I've had the honor to work with at Manuscripts LLC.

Finally, thank you, Renette. Every time we looked at each other and said, "This needs to be a book," I took note. You and I know all the words of the story. This book would never have been written without your loyalty and support. And the journey wouldn't have been the same without you.

Appendix

INTRODUCTION

Williams, Victoria. 2021. *Small Business Facts: Women-Owned Employer Businesses.* Washington DC: US Small Business Administration Office of Advocacy.

CHAPTER 1—BARBIE DREAM HOUSE

Barbie. 2023. "About Barbie." Facebook, May 23, 2003, 7:15 p.m. https://www.facebook.com/barbie/about_details.

Macbride, Elizabeth. 2019. "Successful Women Are Starting Businesses. Yes, Even After 50." *Forbes* (blog), *Forbes*. June 24, 2019. https://www.forbes.com/sites/elizabethmacbride/2019/06/24/women-entrepreneurs-get-better-with-age/?sh=5c0788cd-doab.

CHAPTER 2—CLIENT PROBLEMS

Alexander, Tom. 2018. "How to Work Best with the 4 Different Types of Learners." *Atlassian* (blog), *Atlassian*. October 30,

2018. https://www.atlassian.com/blog/teamwork/how-to-work-4-different-learning-types.

CHAPTER 3—PEOPLE MATTER

Global Living Wage Coalition. 2018. "What is a Living Wage." Global Living Wage Coalition. Accessed December 8, 2022. https://globallivingwage.org/about/what-is-a-living-wage/.

Guy. 2021. "Good Company Culture is Good Business." *Business Fitness* (blog), *Business Fitness*. October 5, 2021. https://businessfitness.biz/good-company-culture-is-good-business/.

CHAPTER 4—SERVANT LEADERSHIP

IMD. 2023. "The 6 Most Common Leadership Styles & How to Find Yours." *IMD* (blog), *International Institute for Management Development*. January 2023. https://www.imd.org/reflections/leadership-styles/.

IMD. 2023. "Everything You Need to Know about Servant Leadership." *IMD* (blog), *International Institute for Management Development*. January 2023. https://www.imd.org/reflections/servant-leadership/.

Greenleaf, Robert. 2015. *"The Servant as Leader."* Atlanta, GA: The Greenleaf Center for Servant Leadership.

Glasmeier, Amy. 2023. "Living Wage Calculator." *Massachusetts Institute of Technology*. February 1, 2023. https://livingwage.mit.edu/articles/103-new-data-posted-2023-living-wage-calculator.

US Bureau of Labor Statistics. *A Profile of the Working Poor.* Washington DC: US Bureau of Labor Statistics. July 2020. https://www.bls.gov/opub/reports/working-poor/2018/home.htm.

CHAPTER 5—BLEEDING EDGE SYNDROME

A-1 Performance Auto. 2020. "Most Common Problems with Nissan Leaf 1st Generation." *A-1 Performance Auto* (blog), *A-1 Performance Auto.* February 20, 2020. https://a1performanceautorepair.com/most-common-problems-with-nissan-leaf-1st-generation/.

Chandler, Jennifer. 2017. "Kim Heathcott, Founder & CEO of Clarion Security: FACES of Memphis." *StyleBlueprint* (blog), *StyleBlueprint.* October 22, 2017. https://styleblueprint.com/memphis/everyday/kim-heathcott-founder-ceo-clarion-security-faces-memphis/.

Neftegaz.Ru. 2021. "Cutting-Edge Technology." *Neftegaz.Ru* (blog), *Neftegaz.Ru.* February 3, 2021. https://neftegazru.com/tech-library/technology/663211-cutting-edge-technology/.

Oxford Languages. 2023. *Oxford Languages.* United Kingdom: Oxford University Press.

Williamson, Will. 2019. "Stand Out from Your Competitors." *JDR group* (blog), *JDR group.* December 19, 2019. https://www.jdrgroup.co.uk/blog/stand-out-from-your-competitors/.

CHAPTER 6—FINANCIAL CRISIS

Ah-Lim, Annabel. 2023. "Calculate the Working Capital Cycle of your Business." *Just Entrepreneurs* (blog), *Just Entrepreneurs*. January 15, 2023. https://justentrepreneurs.co.uk/blog/calculate-the-working-capital-cycle-for-your-business/.

CFI Team. 2023. "Burn Rate. The Rate of Depletion of a Company's Cash Pool." *Corporate Finance Institute* (blog), CFI Education INC. June 28, 2023. https://corporatefinanceinstitute.com/resources/accounting/burn-rate/.

Churchill, Neil, and John Mullins. 2001. "How Fast Can Your Company Afford to Grow?" *Harvard Business Review*. May 2001. https://hbr.org/2001/05/how-fast-can-your-company-afford-to-grow.

Salvucci, Jeremy. 2023. "What is a Leverage Ratio? Definition, Calculation and Examples." *The Street* (blog), *TheStreet*. February 2, 2023. https://www.thestreet.com/dictionary/l/leverage-ratio.

US Small Business Administration. 2023. "Loans." 2023. https://www.sba.gov/funding-programs/loans.

US Small Business Administration. 2023. "Investment Capital." SBA (blog), SBA. May 19, 2023. https://www.sba.gov/funding-programs/investment-capital/.

CHAPTER 7—PROPERTY PERILS

Davidson, Morris. 2023. "Can You Make an Employee Pay for Damages?" *DavidsonMorris* (blog), DavidsonMorris. June

15, 2023. https://www.davidsonmorris.com/can-you-make-an-employee-pay-for-damages/.

PaperTrails. 2023. "What to do When an Employee Destroys Company Property." *Papertrails* (blog), *PaperTrails*. 2023. https://www.papertrails.com/what-to-do-when-an-employee-destroys-company-property/.

PaperTrails. 2023. "Termination Meeting: Mistakes to Avoid." *Papertrails* (blog), *PaperTrails*. 2023. https://www.papertrails.com/termination-meeting-mistakes-to-avoid/.

CHAPTER 8: ICE WARS

Maxwell, John. 2020. "How John Maxwell's Law of Mount Everest Can Help Us Through Self-Isolation." *hcleadershipessentials* (blog), HarperCollins Publishers. March 25, 2020. https://hcleadershipessentials.com/blogs/team-development/how-john-maxwells-law-of-mount-everest-can-help-us-through-selfisolation/.

National Weather Service. n.d. "Ice Storms." *Weather* (blog), *National Weather Service*. n.d. https://www.weather.gov/safety/winter-ice-frost#:~:text=Black%20ice%20can%20also%20form,at%20manmade%20and%20natural%20obstructions.

CHAPTER 9—HOLIDAY MEALS

Grammarist. 2023. "Too Much of a Good Thing." *Grammarist* (blog), Grammarist. 2023. https://grammarist.com/idiom/too-much-of-a-good-thing/#:~:text=Too%20much%20of%20

a%20good%20thing%20means%20an%20excessive%20 amount,mango%20is%20delicious%20and%20nutritious.

Hadley, Malcom. 2015. "Study: The Key to Happiness at Work is Free Snacks." *USA Today* (blog), *USA Today*. September 16, 2015. https://www.usatoday.com/story/money/2015/09/16/study-says-snacks-affect-happiness-at-work/72259746/.

Stange, Jocelyn. 2020. "The Big List of Employee Perks: 45 Perks to Attract and Retain Talent." *Quantum Workplace* (blog), *Quantum Workplace*. September 15, 2020. https://www.quantumworkplace.com/future-of-work/employee-perks.

CHAPTER 10—PARKING LOT WARS

MVMP. 2020. "Using the Avoiding Conflict Resolution Style." *MVMP Mediation* (blog), *MVMP Martha's Vineyard Mediation Program*. April 21, 2020. https://www.mvmediation.org/blog/conflict-resolution-ideas-day-37/.

CHAPTER 11—UNHINGED

Derrow, Paula. 2023. "Everything You Ever Wanted to Know About Stress and How to Manage It." *Everyday Health* (blog), *Everyday Health*. January 1, 2023. https://www.everydayhealth.com/stress/guide/.

Madell, Robin. n.d. "The Supervisor's Impact on Employee Engagement." *Chron* (blog), *Chron*. n.d. https://smallbusiness.chron.com/supervisors-impact-employehttps://smallbusiness.chron.com/supervisors-impact-employee-engagement-14673.htmle-engagement-14673.html.

MasterClass. 2022. "How to Manage Managers: 5 Tips for Managing Managers." *MasterClass* (blog), *MasterClass*. May 17, 2022. https://www.masterclass.com/articles/managing-managers.

MasterClass. 2021. "Understanding KPIs: 12 Types of Key Performance Indicators." *MasterClass* (blog), *MasterClass*. November 2, 2021. https://www.masterclass.com/articles/key-performance-indicators-explained.

Strauch, Ingrid and Lauren Bedosky. 2022. "How to Avoid an Emotional Meltdown, and What to Do When It Happens Anyway." *Everyday Health* (blog), *Everyday Health*. June 17, 2023. https://www.everydayhealth.com/wellness/united-states-of-stress/emotional-meltdowns-why-they-happen-how-prevent-them/.

Queensland Government, Queensland. 2015. "Fractured Rocks." *Wetland Info*. https://wetlandinfo.des.qld.gov.au/wetlands/ecology/aquatic-ecosystems-natural/groundwater-dependent/fractured-rocks/.

CHAPTER 12—UNDER PRESSURE

Bhandari, Smitha. 2022. WebMD. "What Does Stress Do to the Body?" *WebMD* (blog), *Web MD*. December 16, 2022. https://www.webmd.com/balance/stress-management/stress-and-the-body.

Harvard Health Publishing. 2020. "Understanding the Stress Response." *Harvard Health*. (blog), *Harvard Health Pub-*

lishing. July 6, 2020. https://www.health.harvard.edu/staying-healthy/understanding-the-stress-response/.

Valcour, Monique. 2016. "Beating Burnout." *Harvard Business Review*. May 2016. https://hbr.org/2016/11/beating-burnout.

CHAPTER 13—PERFECTIONISM, PERSONALITY, AND PREDICAMENTS

16 Personalities. "Defender Personality, ISFJ-A/ISFJ-T. What's the Difference?" *16 Personalities* (blog), *16 Personalities*. 2023. https://www.16personalities.com/isfj-personality.

Discprofile. 2023. "What is DiSC? Deepen your Understanding of Yourself and Others." *Discprofile* (blog), Personality Profile Solutions, LLC. 2023. https://www.discprofile.com/what-is-disc/.

Johns, Damon. 2018. "Which Personality Type Makes the Best CEO?" *Medium* (Blog), *Medium*. Oct 29, 2018. https://medium.com/@nextlevelsuccess/which-personality-type-makes-the-best-ceo-daymond-johns-success-formula-6af744c5579a.

Mannarino, Meghan. 2023. "Four Signs It May Be Time to Seek Professional Health." *Forbes* (blog), *Forbes*. May 4, 2023. https://www.forbes.com/health/mind/professional-mental-help/.

MyPersonality. 2023. "Commander. ENTJ." *MyPersonality* (blog), *My personality*. 2023. https://mypersonality.net/personality-type/entj.

Nied, Jennifer. 2022. "What's the Enneagram Test? Plus, What to Do with Your Results." *Shape* (blog), *Shape*. November 10, 2022. https://www.shape.com/lifestyle/mind-and-body/what-is-enneagram-test/.

Owens, Molly. 2021. "Enneagram Type 1—the Perfectionist." *Truity* (blog), *Truity*. 2021. https://www.truity.com/enneagram/personality-type-1-perfectionist/.

Santilli, Mara. 2023. "How to Stop Overthinking: Causes and Ways to Cope." *Forbes* (blog), *Forbes*. 2023. https://www.forbes.com/health/mind/what-causes-overthinking-and-6-ways-to-stop/.

The Meyers & Briggs Foundation. 2023. "Thinking or Feeling." Adapted from Looking at Type: The Fundamentals by Charles R. Martin (Gainesville, FL: CAPT 1997). https://www.myersbriggs.org/my-mbti-personality-type/mbti-basics/thinking-or-feeling.htm.

Universal Class. 2023. "The Process of Personality Development." *Universal Class* (blog), *Universal Class*. 2023. https://www.universalclass.com/articles/self-help/the-process-of-personality-development.htm.

CHAPTER 14—RANSOMED

Continuity Central. 2022. "Survey Reveals the Important Role of Malicious Insiders in Successful Ransomware Attacks." *Continuity Central* (blog), *Continuity Central*. July 28, 2022. https://www.continuitycentral.com/index.php/news/technology/7544-survey-reveals-the-important-role-of-malicious-in-siders-in-successful-ransomware-attacks.

Horowitz, Daphna. 2020. "Leaders: Put on Your Own Oxygen Mask First." *Forbes* (blog), *Forbes*. June 9, 2020. https://www.forbes.com/sites/forbescoachescouncil/2020/06/09/leaders-put-your-own-oxygen-mask-on-first/?sh=48f2d78377ad.

ID Agent. 2022. "How Do Malicious Insiders Damage Companies." *ID Agent* (blog), *ID Agent*. November 3, 2022. https://www.idagent.com/blog/how-do-malicious-insider-threats-damage-companies/.

Kurter, Heidi Lynne. 2021. "Managers, here are 3 Warning Signs Your Employees Are Burnt Out." *Forbes* (blog), *Forbes*. June 30, 2021. https://www.forbes.com/sites/heidilynnekurter/2021/06/30/managers-here-are-3-warning-signs-your-employees-are-burnt-out/?sh=665ccf93b769.

Smart, David. 2021. "Keeping the Machine Running." *DWS Associates* (blog), *DWS Associates*. February 11, 2021. https://www.dwsassoc.com/post/keeping-the-machine-running.

CHAPTER 15—WINNING MEMPHIS STYLE

Shelby County TN. "Role of the County Commission." *Shelby County TN*. 2023. https://www.shelbycountytn.gov/1208/Role-of-the-Commission.

CHAPTER 16—SCALING THE HEIGHTS

Benchworks. 2019. "Benchworks Named to Inc. 5000 List of America's Fastest-Growing Private Companies for Fifth Year in a Row." *Benchworks* (blog), *Benchworks*. 2023. https://benchworks.com/benchworks-named-to-inc-5000-list-of-americas-fastest-growing-private-companies-for-fifth-year-in-a-row/.

Churchill, Neil C., and Virginia L. Lewis. 1983. "The Five Stages of Small Business Growth." *Harvard Business Review*. May 1983. https://hbr.org/1983/05/the-five-stages-of-small-business-growth.

Soco Sales Management Training. 2023. "Differences Between Hunters and Farmers Explained." *Soco Selling* (blog), Soco Sales Training. 2023. https://www.socoselling.com/finding-hiring-farmer-sales-role/.

Twintel. 2022. "Why Being on the Inc. 5000 List Matters." *Twintel* (blog) *Twintel Team*. August 18, 2022. https://www.twintel.net/business/why-being-on-the-inc-5000-list-matters.

CHAPTER 17—THE PINNACLE

Inc. 5000. "America's Entrepreneurs. 5000 strong." Inc. Accessed April 2, 2023. https://www.inc.com/inc5000/apply.

NAWBO. "About NAWBO, Our Vision and Mission." NAWBO. Accessed May 25, 2023. https://www.nawbo.org/about-nawbo-our-vision-and-mission#:~:text=The%20National%20Association%20of%20Women%20Business%20Owners%20(NAWBO)%20propels%20women,development%-20within%20the%20entrepreneurial%20community.

NAWBO. "NAWBO Awards." NAWBO. Accessed March 15, 2023. https://www.nawbo.org/about/nawbo-awards.

CHAPTER 18—THE DROP

Charles Retina Institute. 2019. "The Society of Entrepreneurs." *Charles Retina Institute* (blog), *Charles Retina Institute*. 2019. https://www.charlesretina.com/society-of-entrepreneurs-2019-inductee/.

Graham, Ciera. 2023. "Avoidance Coping: Is it Okay to Escape through Work?" *Career Contessa* (blog), *Career Contessa*. 2023. https://www.careercontessa.com/advice/avoidance-coping/.

Koretz, Janna. 2019. "What Happens When Your Career Becomes Your Whole Identity." *Harvard Business Review*. December 2019. https://hbr.org/2019/12/what-happens-when-your-career-becomes-your-whole-identity.

SOE Memphis. 2023. "Society of Entrepreneurs." SOE Memphis. Accessed June 3, 2023. https://soememphis.com/.

Stites, Adam. 2018. "Patriots, Eagles Combine to Easily Smash the Record for Yards in a Super Bowl." *SB Nation* (blog), *SB Nation*. February 4, 2018. https://www.sbnation.com/2018/2/4/16972244/patriots-eagles-super-bowl-52-total-yards-record-2018.

CHAPTER 19—KUDZU

CEO Today. 2021. "5 Tips for Running a Business with Your Spouse." *CEO Today Magazine* (blog), *CEO Today*. April 4, 2021. https://www.ceotodaymagazine.com/2021/04/5-tips-for-running-a-business-with-your-spouse/.

CHAPTER 20—DECISIONS

Churchill, Neil C., and Virginia L. Lewis. 1983. "The Five Stages of Small Business Growth." *Harvard Business Review*. May 1983. https://hbr.org/1983/05/the-five-stages-of-small-business-growth.

Hinkel, Sadie. 2022. "The Importance of Boundaries and Saying No." *The Kim Foundation* (blog), *The Kim Foundation*. August 10, 2022. https://thekimfoundation.org/the-importance-of-setting-boundaries-saying-no/.

Ye, Leslie. 2018. "The Psychology of Choice: How to Make Easier Decisions." *HubSpot* (blog), *HubSpot*. August 15, 2018. https://blog.hubspot.com/sales/the-psychology-of-choice.

CHAPTER 21—REINVENTION

Hall, Ali. 2023. "5 Helpful Tips to Start Over in Life and Begin Again." *Tracking Happiness* (blog), *TRACKING HAPPINESS*. January 9, 2023. https://www.trackinghappiness.com/how-to-start-over/.

CHAPTER 22—REFRESHMENT

Chernoff, Angel. 2023. "10 Life Lessons People Learn Too Late." *Marc and Angel* (blog), *Marc and Angel Hack Life*. May 23, 2023. https://www.marcandangel.com/2023/05/23/10-life-lessons-people-learn-too-late/.

Chernoff, Marc, and Angel Chernoff. 2018. *Getting Back to Happy*. New York, NY: Penguin Random House.

Coursera. 2023. "The Science of Well Being." *Coursera* (blog), *Coursera*. 2023. https://www.coursera.org/learn/the-science-of-well-being.

Elassar, Alaa. 2022. "Two years into the Pandemic, Yale's 'Happiness' Course is More Popular Than Ever." *CNN* (blog). *CNN*. January 23, 2022. https://www.cnn.com/2022/01/23/us/yale-happiness-course-pandemic-wellness/index.html.

Marc and Angel Hack Life. 2023. "About Mark and Angel Hack Life". *Marc and Angel* (blog), *Marc and Angel Hack Life*. 2023. https://www.marcandangel.com/about/.

Santos, Laurie. 2020. "Laurie Santos, Yale Happiness Professor, on 5 Things That Will Make You Happier." *Newsweek* (blog), *Newsweek*. December 12, 2020. https://www.newsweek.com/2021/01/08/laurie-santos-yale-happiness-professor-5-things-that-will-make-you-happier-1556182.html.

CHAPTER 23- REFLECTIONS

Masterson, Victoria. 2022. "Here's What Women's Entrepreneurship Looks Like Around the World." *weforum* (blog), *World*

Economic Forum. July 20, 2022 https://www.weforum.org/agenda/2022/07/women-entrepreneurs-gusto-gender/.

McIntyre, Georgia. 2020. "What Percentage of Small Businesses Fail? (And Other Need-to-Know Stats)." *Fundera* (blog), *Fundera*. November 20, 2020. https://www.fundera.com/blog/what-percentage-of-small-businesses-fail.

Deane, Michael T. 2022. "Top 6 Reasons New Businesses Fail." *Investopedia* (blog), *Investopedia*. December 30, 2022. https://www.investopedia.com/financial-edge/1010/top-6-reasons-new-businesses-fail.aspx.

Eisenmann, Tom. 2021. "Why Start-ups Fail. It's Not Always the Horse or the Jockey." *Harvard Business Review.* May-June 2021. https://hbr.org/2021/05/why-start-ups-fail.

Skok, David. 2010. Matrix Partners. "6 Reasons Startups Fail." *for Entrepreneurs* (blog), Matrix Management Corporation. 2010. https://www.forentrepreneurs.com/why-startups-fail/.

Made in the USA
Coppell, TX
05 December 2023